C000080988

"In this book the wonders o
through the eyes of six high
fascinating insights, the bo
way that is accessible to th
background. A highly reco

Dr Denis R. Alexander, Emeritus Director, The Faraday Institute, Cambridge

"This book entices the reader with engaging personal stories, and exciting scientific findings. Along the way we meet several scientists, hearing their stories of the challenges of science and of the joys of discovery, and learn how science fits with their Christian faith. Readers are invited to revel in the wonders of the natural world and to ponder the larger 'why' questions that science alone can't answer, such as meaning, beauty, and God. A great book for science fans, pastors, and students."

Dr Deborah Haarsma, Astronomer and President of BioLogos

"This is a wonderful book about wonder. In the presence of the world's top scientists this will lead you into a new excitement with and appreciation of the natural world. And for some, it may lead to worship."

Revd Professor David Wilkinson, Principal of St John's College, Durham

"This book by Ruth M. Bancewicz really draws us into the excitement of scientific discovery. It's a lively combination of cutting-edge research and the personal stories of scientists, both of which show us how science and faith can be friends not foes, each in their own way leading us into the wonder of the world we live in. A great read for a young adult and a great gift too for anyone wondering how faith and science fit together."

Rt Revd Dr David Thompson, former Bishop of Huntingdon

"*Wonders of the Living World* explores scientific discovery and its interaction with beliefs in a fresh and much-needed way: not simply through reasoned argument, but also by awakening the imagination and instilling a sense of awe. Bancewicz deftly considers how the beauty and intricacy in nature, uncovered by scientific pursuit, is helpful in addressing questions of ultimate meaning and purpose. I highly recommend it!"

Dr Sharon Dirckx, Oxford Centre for Christian Apologetics, and author of *Am I Just My Brain?*

"When I picked up this book, I couldn't put it down. On every page another wonder of the natural world was beautifully described. The explanations are mixed in with the personal stories of scientists, providing a front-row seat to the excitement of new discovery."

Ard Louis, Professor of Theoretical Physics, University of Oxford

WONDERS
OF THE
LIVING
WORLD

CURIOSITY, AWE, AND
THE MEANING OF LIFE

RUTH M. BANCEWICZ

LION

Text copyright © 2021 Ruth M. Bancewicz
This edition copyright © 2021 Lion Hudson IP Limited

The right of Ruth M. Bancewicz to be identified as the author of this work has been asserted by her in accordance with the Copyright, Designs and Patents Act 1988. All rights reserved. No part of this publication may be reproduced or transmitted in any form or by any means, electronic or mechanical, including photocopy, recording, or any information storage and retrieval system, without permission in writing from the publisher.

Published by
Lion Hudson Limited
Wilkinson House
Jordan Hill Business Park
Banbury Road, Oxford OX2 8DR
England
www.lionhudson.com

ISBN colour hardback 978 0 7459 8054 6
ISBN black-white 978 0 7459 8129 1
e-ISBN 978 0 7459 8128 4

First edition 2021

Acknowledgements
Scripture quotations taken from the Holy Bible, New International Version Anglicised. Copyright © 1979, 1984, 2011 Biblica, formerly International Bible Society. Used by permission of Hodder & Stoughton Ltd, an Hachette UK company. All rights reserved. "NIV" is a registered trademark of Biblica. UK trademark number 1448790.
Scripture quotations marked "MSG" taken from The Message.Copyright © by Eugene H. Peterson 1993, 1994, 1995, 1996, 2000, 2001, 2002.Used by permission of NavPress Publishing Group.

A catalogue record for this book is available from the British Library

Printed and bound in the United Kingdom, March 2021, LH57

Contents

Chapter 1

Exploring the Wonders of the Living World: An introduction

The internet was not the first major network on earth. Underneath the ground in any healthy forest are literally tonnes of fungi growing around the roots of the trees. These partner-organisms share nutrients with the trees, occasionally popping up a fruiting body or mushroom to release their spores into the wider world. The fungi spread so far that they connect the trees together, so nutrients are not just shared between a single sapling and the fungus growing on its roots, but also between one tree and another. The interconnectedness of the network can be measured in a simple experiment in which a traceable substance fed to one tree shows up in the roots of another tree elsewhere in the network.

This link between trees and their fungi is a great example of science revealing aspects of the world that would otherwise be completely hidden to us. As we start to understand how things work, our initial curiosity may lead to surprise, fascination, and a more lasting sense of wonder.

This book explores seven different aspects of the living world, starting with the microscopic and gradually zooming out to whole ecosystems. Each chapter is a story in itself, demonstrating the great beauty and wonder of our planet and the organisms that make their home on it. Together, these stories paint a picture of a place that is fruitful, ordered, and bursting with potential for many different kinds of life.

Our journey begins with a tour of the inner world of the cell, and the secret recipes for growth and development that are hidden inside its biological libraries. The chemical language of life has amazing properties: as a system for storing and passing on biological information, it may be one in a million. We see the constant movement of tiny molecules coming together like the dots in an impressionist's painting to make up a complete cell. Then, on a slightly larger scale, we look at how groups of cells can work together, multiplying and moving in a highly coordinated dance as they grow from an embryo into a newborn baby.

From here we explore how, over a long period of time, organisms hit upon new solutions to the challenges of life on earth. Different species often find similar ways to thrive, as if they were following well-worn paths in a map of life. One of the most important survival techniques is working together. From single cells to whole organisms, living things "snuggle" for existence. At the very largest scale, whole ecosystems are like living cities, providing homes and services to millions of different organisms.

As we step back and take in the big picture, our sense of wonder in discovery can turn to awe as we observe the scale and complexity of the living world. When we understand more about our surroundings, we also start to ask new questions. Each topic in this book has been chosen because it touches at the heart of who we are as human beings, raising questions about meaning and purpose. What's so special about life? Why are we here? Where is it all heading?

Many of these questions can be tackled at a scientific level, but they also point to areas of knowledge that lie beyond science. The scientists who have contributed their thoughts to this book are all people of faith who take these sorts of discussions very seriously. They believe that their work is consistent with the existence of the God of the Bible, so toward the end we will also explore how their views fit in with Christian theology.

Each reader will approach questions of science, meaning, and purpose in a different way. Some may be fairly sure that God exists, and others might not. Many Christians will be confident that the book of Genesis speaks in theological and not scientific terms, so there is no problem with a Christian accepting evolutionary biology. Others may take a different view. The aim of this book is not to cover the issue of creation and evolution in depth, because others have already done that in helpful ways. This book is just an introduction –

which will be enough for some, but frustratingly brief for others. The further reading section provides a list of books for readers who want to follow up these topics in more depth (pages 99–101).

Our aim here is simply to showcase the work of six scientists so you can share their sense of wonder and awe, and begin to think about the questions of meaning and purpose that they are asking – including the ultimate question of what this planet is for. We hope that you find this journey through the living world fascinating, exciting, and inspiring.

Chapter 2

Inner Worlds: A tour of the inner workings of a cell

I have always loved finding out how things work. Some of my favourite books as a child were the ones with lots of detailed pictures and cross-sections. Whatever the topic – castles or Romans, cars or boats – each page was a riot of information I could pore over for hours. There was always a bit of introductory text, but the best parts were the labels showing what people did, how machines worked, or what happened in different sections of a building. There were often little cartoons down the side of the page showing what life was like for the people involved, complete with funny or disgusting details. Exploring these books was a way of experiencing worlds I could never see for myself.

In my last couple of years at secondary school, I found I could apply this love of information and visual detail by studying biology. I got to look at things up close and find out what every part did. I was able to draw my own cross-section diagrams and add my own labels. There wasn't much creativity going on yet, but it was great to be exploring things in more depth.

Life became even more interesting at university. For example, I had already learned at school about the eardrum and the collection of tiny bones that pass the sound waves into the fluid in your inner ear. I loved delving even deeper inside, finding out that those transmitted waves vibrate a tiny membrane, which wobbles some even tinier hairs, which trigger some nerve endings, which fire a signal to the brain. The deeper the tone of the sound, the further it has to travel down the ear to be detected – which is why I found it harder to pitch the low notes on my violin.

I was amazed to find that anyone could know about processes like this so comprehensively, right down to the chemicals involved in sending signals from one part of the body to another. Compared to my cutaway book experiences, four years of intensive study in biology took me way past the pictures and right into the middle of things, where I could explore them for myself.

Before I could explore the inner world of living organisms for myself, I had to learn how to do my own lab-based research. In the same way that a jump from books to real castles would involve acquiring some archaeological skills, I also had a lot to learn – but I found that exciting rather than intimidating. There was a point in my studies, perhaps in my second or third year at university, when I became aware that I was being taught right up to the limits of what was known at the time. I realized that the details and the information in science are always changing as people learn more and more about how things work. So, as a researcher, I could be involved in writing the books.

I was also completely hooked by the creative methods people were using to understand what goes on inside living things. Using relatively simple organisms like yeast or tiny roundworms, scientists are able to pick out individual molecules or processes and study them up close. Fluorescent dyes help us visualize what is going on, so research presentations are not just very visual – they can also look like a work of art.

Another useful technique in biology is to study what happens when something goes wrong. Sometimes it's easier to find out how a machine works by taking out one of the cogs, and in a sense that's what happens when an organism has an inherited disease. By studying these types of problems in relatively simple animals like fruit flies or worms, we can find out how the same or similar processes work in our own bodies.

I wanted to dive into this kind of research as soon as possible, so I signed up for another few years at university as a postgraduate student. With the microscope technology now available to me, my view of the world was suddenly expanded downward. I was finally exploring at a level that allowed me to experience the world of the cell in a way that felt almost first-hand. I studied bacteria and yeast, and saw delicate fish embryos develop over a period of just a few hours. I grew human cells in a dish (getting a fright when one day they had turned into beating heart cells), and learned how to mark different types of cell with chemical dyes.

This chapter explores the inner world of the cell, looking at how the instructions to build it are transmitted from one generation to another. It also looks at my own research on what happens when that process goes wrong. The rest of the book builds on this foundation, revelling in some of the things that are being revealed through science, and asking the questions these discoveries raise about meaning and purpose.

A castle is full of different rooms. Each space has its own furniture or equipment and is inhabited by particular people – or even animals. In a similar way, all living things are made of one or more cells, which are connected like rooms in a palace. Most cells are far too small to see with the naked eye, but eggs are an exception to this rule. For example, an unfertilized chicken's egg contains one huge single cell, and a human egg is about 0.1 mm wide, so is just about visible if the light is good. Most other types of cell are so small that scientists had to invent microscopes before they could discover that our bodies are actually a mosaic of tiny compartments.

Your own body is a collection of around 30 trillion (30,000,000,000,000) cells, each of which is joined to its neighbours with the molecular equivalent of plastic clothes fasteners, or sometimes pipes. Some cells produce substances that cushion or protect them from their surroundings, or solidify into bone or cartilage. These different materials are stuck to each other with a glue-like substance, so the end result is a robust body that can move around easily and withstand a fair amount of impact.

Cells themselves are essentially flexible bags stuffed to the brim with a syrupy mixture of life-giving ingredients (see figure 1, page 106). Each one contains billions of molecules and molecular machines, and hundreds of specialized compartments. These parts are not static because, like a room in a castle, the inside of a cell is a busy place where it makes or processes everything it needs to stay alive and do its part in the body. When parts are worn out or no longer needed, they are broken down or recycled, and replaced with new ones.

Most of the work in a cell happens inside small sub-compartments, each of which has its own specialist function. Structural support is provided by a kind of scaffolding called the cytoskeleton, which also acts as rails for transporting things around, or helps the cell itself to move around (see Chapter 4). In a sense, each cell is as complex as a whole castle, and your body is a collection of them added together.

An ancient castle is full of workers that run from place to place, in and out of different rooms, and up and down the scaffolding. Others stay put, doing their day-to-day work in one specific location. Each type of worker has been chosen and trained for a particular role and is managed by a particular person. There are soldiers and stable hands, cooks and washers up, chambermaids, pageboys, and so on.

The cell operates in a similar way. Most of the workers are molecules called proteins, and each one belongs to a specialized group with its own role. Transport proteins cart things around the cell, and enzymes speed up chemical reactions. Hormones carry signals, which are picked up by receptor proteins. Some proteins defend the cell, while others store things away for leaner times. Structural proteins give shape and support, and motility proteins help the cell to glide around. All of these processes are coordinated by regulatory proteins, which are the project managers of the cell.

The hub of any castle is probably its kitchen. This is possibly the busiest room and also one of the largest. A huge range of food is made here: rich and varied for the owners and their noble guests, and simple and filling for the servants and soldiers. Without the kitchen and the food it produces, the activity in a castle would soon come to a halt.

For a cell, the main centre of activity is its nucleus, but this is more like a library than a kitchen. All the instructions for building every protein in the cell, in the right place at the right time, are kept in one large compartment. In a sense this information is like a collection of recipes, and they are contained in code form in the molecule of deoxyribonucleic acid, or DNA.

Your own DNA contains about 20,000 recipes, spelled out in a code with just four letters: A, T, C, and G. These characters represent the four chemical building blocks of the DNA molecule: Adenine, Thymine, Cytosine, and Guanine. A and T fit together as a pair, and so do C and G. (If you have just one side of the DNA double helix, you can predict the other, which is exactly what the cell does when it copies its DNA – see page 14.)

In the same way that we use the twenty-six letters of the English alphabet to make thousands of words and countless different sentences, our bodies use four chemical letters to make "words" that together produce recipes known as genes. DNA words are three letters long, so the number of words available is fewer than in the English language,[1] but they are enough to build a body.

To make a protein, the DNA-reading machinery of the cell skims down one side of the double helix, copying out a short section. That coded message is then sent out of the nucleus for translation. Each word in the code corresponds to one building block in a protein, which is called an amino acid. As the cell's translating machinery slides down the message, it adds those building blocks together like beads on a string (see figure 2, page 106). The string is then folded up into its own particular shape: a finished protein ready to do its work in the cell.

Getting to grips with the inner life of something as complex as a cell can be mind-boggling at times, but it can also be incredibly awe-inspiring. For example, the average human cell is between ten and a hundred times smaller than a millimetre, and its nucleus contains two metres of DNA. That feat of packaging is the equivalent of trying to put 700 kilometres of strong thread into a bath, without tangles, and with the ability to find any given section when needed. The solution would be to wrap the thread around a series of bobbins, and that is exactly what happens in the cell.

If you took all the DNA out of your body and stretched it out end to end, how far would it reach? This sum is fairly simple – two metres times the number of cells in your body – but the second number is difficult to pin down. The most recent estimates give a figure of around 30 trillion (30,000,000,000) cells in the average adult's body. The latest counts show that around 10 per cent of these cells still contain DNA, and the other 90 per cent are red blood cells and platelets, which destroy their DNA to make room for oxygen-carrying haemoglobin or blood-clotting factors.

With at least 3 trillion DNA-containing cells, and two metres of DNA in each cell, your body contains at least 6 billion (6,000,000,000)

---

1   With four choices for each letter, the total number of possible three-letter code words is $4 \times 4 \times 4 = 64$.

kilometres of DNA. The sun is about 150 million kilometres from earth, so the DNA in your body could take you there and back at least twenty times. If you didn't mind going on a one-way trip, it could take you all the way from Earth to Pluto.

The inner world of the cell is fantastically complicated, from DNA to a body packed full of molecular machinery. So much could go wrong, but the biology of the cell is a very robust system that works nearly every time. My own research involved homing in on those unfortunate times when one particular cog in the protein-making machine is broken – especially when that fault is caused by a problem in the DNA code.

A baby born to thirty-year-old parents has, on average, around ninety completely new spelling mistakes in its DNA. That may sound like a lot, but it's amazing that the number is as low as it is. The gametes (sperm and eggs) that make a baby are produced in pretty much the same way as every other type of cell: by splitting in two.[2] Every time a cell divides, it manufactures a complete copy of its entire contents, including its DNA. Your own two metres of DNA is 6 billion subunits long, and replicating that is the equivalent of writing out the text of this book more than 30,000 times. The process of DNA copying is amazingly accurate, and has built-in proofreading mechanisms, but every now and then a typo, called a mutation, slips through.

Most of the mistakes in a new baby's DNA won't have any impact on its health. A mutation often doesn't cause any real changes in a protein, but even if it does, the child might still be OK. Our DNA is divided into forty-six sections, called chromosomes, which come as twenty-three matching pairs. One half of each pair comes from our mother and the other is from our father, so there is a spare copy of every gene.[3]

Occasionally, a mutation might cause problems. For example, both copies of a gene (the mother's and the father's) might be needed to make the correct amount of protein. Or perhaps one copy was

2   For gametes there is an extra division that separates the chromosome pairs; otherwise you would inherit two copies of a chromosome from each parent instead of one and have far too much DNA (see page 35).
3   Except for genes on the twenty-third pair of chromosomes: the sex chromosomes. With two different sex chromosomes – X and Y – males have some non-matching genes.

already damaged. Most harmful mutations will have a fairly general effect, like contributing to an increased susceptibility to diabetes or heart disease, where the outcome can often be improved by a healthy lifestyle. Very occasionally, a cog is removed from a vital process and disrupts the body's normal development, and that is what I studied in my own research.

Every family has its historian – the one who keeps track of who's who; whether they're married, have kids, or are single; what they do for a living; and where they live. Genetics is essentially the study of family trees and involves some detective work to connect what's visible on the outside of an organism with what's going on inside. It's a bit like a historian visiting a family's archives, but also spending time in their home rummaging in the cupboards or sitting in a corner watching how things are done on a day-to-day basis.

I began my own research in genetics by investigating the lives of a family of small, stripy zebrafish which had problems with their eyes. Many of them had irregular lenses or corneas, some had differently shaped pupils, and a few had smaller eyes than usual. My hope was that these fish would help me to answer some particular questions about the inner life of animals – most importantly, "Which gene is causing this problem?" and "What can this teach me about normal eye development?"

The disease I was studying had such a clear pattern of inheritance, I was sure that it was caused by a mistake in just one gene. The only problem was, there are so many genes involved in eye development that I couldn't just take a guess. So when some gene-mapping experts offered to help me track down the source of the disease, I jumped at the chance and immediately sent them some samples.

My new colleagues compared the DNA of the healthy and affected fish and tracked the location of the mutation down to a "small" 2-million-subunit-long section on chromosome number seven. My mission now was to figure out which gene in that chunk of DNA might be affected. Which cog in the machine was broken? Other scientists had already created a detailed map of the zebrafish genome, so I used an online database to check the section I was interested in. The most obvious candidate was the *pax6* gene, which is extremely important in eye development, and that is where we finally found the mutation.

My colleagues and I had rummaged inside the cell's inner library of information and found a typo. A single innocuous-looking spelling mistake seemed to have caused a problem in the cell's machine: a cog that was missing, broken, or out of place. We still had to check whether this mutation was really causing the eye problems, and if so, why? I now had to hunt through this fish family's cupboards to find out what had gone wrong.

Nearly everyone else in the lab where I was working was already studying the *pax6* gene in different organisms, so they helped me to check the exact details of the mutation. They also helped me figure out how a single spelling mistake in that gene might mean it can no longer produce a fully functioning protein. After more than a year of work, our experiments finally confirmed my hunch that *pax6* was the faulty cog. So much was already known about this gene and the protein it makes that, as soon as the mutation was confirmed, we could instantly connect the signs of disease on the outside of the animal with the inner world of the cell in quite a bit of detail.

The Pax6 protein is essentially a central cog that controls the activity of a whole cascade of other genes. These genes are hugely important in the formation of the eye, nervous system, and pancreas, and Pax6 switches them on or off in the right places in the body, at the right times. In fact, Pax6 is so vital for normal healthy development that a mistake in just one copy of the gene is usually fatal. The surprising thing about my fish was that they were only affected when both copies of the gene were broken, and even then their condition wasn't fatal. It turns out that zebrafish are better off than most other animals because they have two separate pairs of *pax6* genes which are nearly identical: *pax6a* and *pax6b*. We had found a mutation that mostly inactivated *pax6b*, but *pax6a* was still intact. It is always good to find a mildly affected mutant, because the door is now wide open to study what it does in the human body. Scientists around the world are now able to build on this work, discovering more about how eyes develop and why things sometimes go wrong.

The inner workings of the cell are wonderfully complex, as my own research showed, but the even greater wonder is that we can explore and understand them using the tools of science. I am constantly amazed at how resourceful scientists are at finding new ways to understand what's going on at such minute scales. Our knowledge is continually being revised and updated, with the hope that we are always growing in our understanding of the living world.

The same concept applies to every other field of science, from particle physics to astronomy. We scrutinize each other's work, trying to spot mistakes and the best lines of reasoning. New techniques allow us to delve even deeper into the detail and uncover previously unknown aspects of the processes we study. We know so much more about the world than we did fifty years ago, but who knows what we will find in the next few decades?

Any new discovery raises even more questions than it answers. Many of these questions are scientific, but some stretch beyond science into other areas of knowledge. We see meaning and purpose behind things, and cannot stop asking questions like "Why?" and "What for?" Some of these more philosophical or theological questions can even drive science forward, not just in the direction of useful technologies, but also into new areas of research.

The rest of this book is an exploration of a number of areas of science that raise interesting questions. The people doing this research are motivated by their thirst for knowledge in every area of life – not just science – so the deeper implications of their work will be explored in Chapters 9 and 10. One of the most fundamental questions is, "What is so special about life?", and that is where we'll start in our investigation of the wonders of the living world.

Chapter 3

One in a Million? The chemistry of life in the universe

Some people have a knack for code breaking, but for most of us, staring at one half of a coded message would be a completely pointless exercise – a page of symbols or jumbled-up letters that says absolutely nothing. But suddenly, when we have a key that matches the symbols or letters to words in a language we understand, that code becomes a very powerful thing. Like the Egyptologist who learns to read hieroglyphics, a whole world is suddenly laid open for us to explore.

When the DNA double helix was discovered, it was obvious that the different subunits could be used like letters to spell out a message. The inner world of the cell was waiting to be revealed; the only problem was cracking the code. So after Watson and Crick announced the structure of DNA in 1953, groups of scientists were racing to come up with the key. After a little more than ten years of hard work, the code was finally cracked and they were able to decipher messages that had been hidden since life began.

The information hidden deep in the DNA of any organism is really a series of recipes. Decoding starts when a string of three-letter "words" in the double helix are read off by the cell's machinery and translated into a sequence of amino acids which is folded up into a protein (see figure 2, page 106). Our living bodies are, in essence, a network of interacting proteins – haemoglobin, insulin, and all the rest – that are all made in this way.

The genetic code is the one and only example in biology of two different chemical languages (DNA and protein) that are connected

18

together by a process of translation. The question is, where did this information-storing and sharing system come from, and is it the only one out there?

This chapter is about the origin of the genetic code, and what makes it so special. Some of us might feel there is purpose in the universe, but does that intuition make sense when we look at the science? This isn't about looking for evidence for God, but exploring the biochemistry of life. What can these molecules tell us about our origins, and what questions do they raise about meaning and purpose in the universe?

Ever since he was a student at Cambridge University, Professor Stephen Freeland has been fascinated by the origin of life. He investigates the genetic code with computer-based experiments and simulations, asking how and why it developed as it did. How unique are the molecules of life, and where do they come from? Do they have to be this way? If there is life on other planets, should we expect it to be built from the same chemicals as is life on earth?

As the son of an ordained minister and a Christian himself, Stephen is also interested in the more philosophical questions that his work raises. For example, if the origin of life was inevitable, what does that say about the existence of God? He believes that science is a route to understanding the mechanisms of the universe, while faith answers much bigger questions about creation, meaning, and purpose. Both ways of looking at the world are important, and each can encourage the other. Science inspires questions about God, and theology leads to questions about science. This chapter explores Stephen's questions about the molecules of life from a scientific point of view, but also raises some deeper questions that should not be ignored.

The first clue that there might be something unique about the genetic code is that it is so widely used. If two people were found to be encrypting and deciphering messages in exactly the same way, we would assume they had copied their code from the same source. In the same way, every single organism that has been studied so far – from whales to bacteria – has been found to be using exactly the same system of DNA, protein, and translation machinery.

There may have been a time when other, very different, codes existed, but we have no evidence today of what they might have been.

If there were other ways of storing and sharing information, they died out for one reason or another. So the shared genetic code is clearly a successful solution to the problem of storing and passing on the recipes of life. But is it the best, or just good enough?

The second sign that our genetic code may be something special comes from the way our proteins are built. Construction kits usually come with lots of different parts, covering a range of shapes and sizes. Some are for building the overall structure, and others have more specialized roles. There is normally a selection of colours, or different materials. A really useful set of building blocks has a wide enough range of pieces to give some flexibility for building different things, but not so many as to be confusing. Some of us spent whole days as children building all sorts of things out of small plastic bricks, and the more bricks you collected, the more you could make.

All living things make their proteins from just twenty different amino acids, each of which has its own shape, size, and chemical properties. There are hundreds of other amino acids, but somehow we use this set of just twenty to build our proteins. One of the questions Stephen has asked in his research is, why are only twenty amino acids used to build pretty much every protein on earth, and why these particular ones? These were not the only building blocks around when life was first emerging, or the most easily available. Is there something special about this particular set?

It turns out that our twenty amino acids are a really useful construction kit. There is a good range of shapes and sizes, as well as properties like electrical charge or behaviour in water. Stephen's research group tested a hundred million alternative sets of amino acids and found that ours was one of the most flexible building kits. Only a few of the chemical properties of amino acids were included in this study, so what might the result be if more were included?

There is a lot more to be done, but these early clues suggest that very few sets of amino acids could be as effective as ours at making proteins. In other words, the standard group of amino acids used by living things may be almost perfectly optimized for building proteins.

This is the property that protects it from making mistakes, and it's the third clue to the unique nature of our genetic code. If you or I sat down to come up with a code language, it might not be the best the world has ever seen. It might be pretty simple to crack, or perhaps encrypting and decrypting messages would be too difficult. Thankfully, the systems that banks use to keep our money safe online today are a million miles away from the ones we might have invented ourselves. The study of code-making (or cryptology) is a serious field of research that has its own academic journal, and biological codes can be nearly as sophisticated. Our genetic code may not be the best for storing your bank details, but it does have a unique property that makes it very useful for living organisms.

When cells multiply, they must replicate all their DNA. Each copy has to be as accurate as possible, but, despite all the cell's amazing proofreading mechanisms, a few mistakes always slip through. Every 30 million subunits or so, a spelling mistake called a mutation happens.

Mutations are not the end of the world because there is some flexibility in the way DNA is translated into protein. This is similar to the way we can read a sentence even if it contenes a few spellin mistekes. It might not look great, but the message still makes sense. The advantage here comes from the different sizes of the DNA and protein alphabets. The four DNA "letters" can be used to make sixty-four three-letter code words, but there are only twenty amino acids. This means that each amino acid can be assigned to a group of words, allowing for a bit of wobble in the system (see figure 3, page 107).[4]

Someone learning English may get their UK and US spelling muddled up, using "color" instead of "colour" in a British English essay, but we know what they mean. In a similar way, several related DNA code words are assigned to one amino acid. If there is a spelling mistake in a gene, then it might not affect the protein it makes. So the genetic code is not just something that happens to work OK, but is a remarkably clever system. What Stephen wanted to know was, exactly how good is this error-protection mechanism? Is it like one built by a clever amateur, which works a bit but isn't the best, or does it seem to have been very precisely optimized?

Stephen and his colleagues tested out DNA's error-protection mechanism by creating a computer program to mix up the assignment

---

4   Three of the code words aren't assigned to an amino acid at all, but signal the end of the gene.

of code words to amino acids, producing thousands of alternative codes. The next stage was to check whether these codes were more or less error-proof than ours. How would they be affected by the most common kinds of mutation? Would the translated proteins be more or less affected by spelling mistakes?

The title of this chapter is "One in a Million", because after Stephen tested a million alternative codes, only one was found that was more resistant to mutations than ours. So technically we are two in a million, but the fact that there may be some even more error-proof codes out there doesn't mean that ours is a failure. In fact, there is something very special about our code. It appears to be a system that will not "just do"; it is an optimized solution to the problem of staying alive.

Mutations are essential to life as we know it. Occasionally a gene is improved in some way by a spelling mistake. That change allows the animal that contains it to thrive and breed more easily, passing that version of the gene on to the next generation. Eventually the new variant might become common in the whole population. This mechanism of change is what allows organisms to adapt to new environments, so a completely mutation-resistant genetic code would actually be a bad thing. Our code seems to allow for enough change to help us adapt, but not so much that positive changes are lost before they can become established.

What if one of Stephen's theoretical codes turns out to be better than ours at resisting errors, while also allowing useful change? Two or three in a million is still pretty special, even if it isn't the ultimate example of optimization. But this chapter is not about the supremacy of our particular form of life on earth. For a Christian, there is no need to look for scientific reasons that we as individuals are unique – in the sense that a parent might tell their child that he or she is one of a kind. Christians already have enough theological reasons to believe that we are important to God in that way.

The sort of specialness that Stephen is interested in here is whether there is a particular potential for life in the universe. Perhaps these clues about the genetic code are a hint that life – and life of a certain kind – was bound to emerge on a suitable planet at some point? If the universe is fruitful in this way, then what philosophical or theological ideas might that be compatible with?

Compared to theoretical alternatives, our genetic code seems to have some unique properties. One day Stephen might be able to move beyond computer models and test his ideas on living systems. His question is, if we find organisms – perhaps single-celled life on another planet or moon in our own solar system – will they share the same system of DNA and protein as us? Even now, there are some clues about what the answer to this question might be.

One of the best places to start looking for answers to Stephen's question is in the night sky. Every chemical element other than hydrogen and helium[5] was made in the intense heat of a star's internal furnace. When a star dies, it releases its atoms into interstellar space as a cloud of dust and gas. These remains can condense again to form a nebula where more stars, as well as rocks, ice, and organic molecules will form: the stuff of planets. This cycle of stellar birth and death is what produced all the elements in the periodic table, including the atoms that are so important for making living things. So we are made of stardust, and the molecules in our bodies are mostly hydrogen, carbon, oxygen, and nitrogen, which are four of the most common atoms in the universe. If life arises elsewhere, it might well be made from the same elements as us.

For stars to be born in the first place, the amount of matter and energy in the universe, the interactions between the particles of an atom, and many other physical forces, seem to be set at precisely the right levels. If there were the tiniest variation in just one of these factors, we would not be here. For example, if the force that holds the particles of carbon together were any weaker, carbon would not form. If it were stronger, all the carbon in the universe would turn into oxygen.

Some people say this "fine-tuning" is evidence that there must be a mind or a God behind the process. Others think it's just a coincidence, or that we will eventually find a physical mechanism that explains why these forces are the way they are. The data can't tell us which conclusion is right, but what we can be confident in saying is that life as we know it is the result of some very specific properties of the universe – and those properties are expected by physicists to be the same on every planet where life could arise.

---

5   These were formed in the first minutes after the Big Bang.

Physics and the chemical elements may be the same across the universe, but what about the molecules of life? There is good evidence that small molecules can form on the surface of asteroids: lumps of rock or metal that are constantly hurtling through the clouds of gas and dust where stars are born. When an asteroid crash-lands on earth as a meteorite, it can be analysed for the chemicals it carries – especially if it lands somewhere relatively sterile like Antarctica.

By studying meteorites, scientists have realized that amino acids and molecules similar to the sugars and DNA subunits in living things may be relatively common in space. Eight of our twenty amino acids have been found on meteorites, and the other twelve can be made from them. So the meteorite route might have been a fruitful way of bringing life-giving molecules to any planet.

The actual origin of life may still be something of a mystery, but we do have a few clues about how it might have happened. Researchers like Rhoda Hawkins, whose work is described in the next chapter, are also beginning to show that larger structures can be assembled through the action of physical forces. By jiggling and bouncing into each other, small molecules can come together to form larger ones. These interactions happen inside cells, but also when substances are mixed together in water.

So we now know that the same forces are likely to be in action across the universe, the same materials are available, and the same molecules and possibly even cells could form on the other earth-like planets that have been identified in our galaxy. There is no reason why at least basic organisms should not exist on other planets in our own solar system. The question is, how similar would they be to life on earth?

A rock pool has a convoluted shape. The force of gravity pulls the water down so that it takes on the contours of the seaweed, small animals, rocks, and other debris underneath. If that water was frozen and lifted away, it would bear the imprint of everything underneath.

A similar principle applies to living things. All the organisms on earth reflect something of their environment. When plants and algae make new molecules, they include minerals from rocks in their local environment. Animals are strong enough to resist the force of gravity and move around. In a sense, an imprint of the universe has been made in biological form. So a scientist should be able to predict at least some of the physical properties of an organism's habitat, by looking only at the organisms themselves.

Looking at things in terms of the genetic code, information is transferred from our surroundings to the molecule of DNA. Although biological evolution takes much longer and is far more complex than the effect of gravity on a pool of water, it has a similar result. A population of organisms living in a particular habitat will accumulate mutations, some of which may improve their survival in that place. There might be newborns with different-coloured fur, shorter legs, a longer tongue, and so on. If a new feature helps the organism to breed more successfully, then the mutation that caused it will spread throughout the population. Over time, those organisms will come to "fit" their environment more and more.

So if earth-like conditions were found on a planet elsewhere in the universe, you might also expect any organisms you came across to look a little similar to those on earth. This principle of life fitting to its surroundings may also have applied to the origin of the genetic code itself. Is our genetic code ideally suited to life on a rocky planet orbiting a smallish star?

When a cryptologist invents a new code, there will be some things they have to bear in mind. Will it be worked out by a computer or by a person? What sort of messages will it be used to send? How will they be sent, and how much time is there for the decoding? How secure should it be? What if there were so many constraints that another cryptologist could predict the sort of code that would be made? They might not get the exact same one, but they might predict whether letters or numbers were used, how many digits, and so on.

Stephen's question about what the genetic code on other planets would be like is a similar puzzle. Would this be an inevitable outcome of the physical properties of the universe? Should we expect to find the same thing on another planet? These are huge questions, and it seems that the answers at the moment are partly yes and partly no.

Organic life is so complex that we cannot say exactly how things will turn out in every situation, but some basic principles could be used to predict what sort of life might emerge on other planets. Many of the conditions on our planet are determined by the physical properties of the universe: gravity, light from the sun, rocks, and so on. These same laws of physics are what produce all the elements in the periodic table, which are available across the universe. Looking at those basic atoms, it's possible to predict some of the molecules that can form and the ways they will behave. The question is, how far does this process of prediction reach forward into biology?

We might be able to predict some of the properties of the genetic code right now, but not all of them. Although, as we've said above, our own code is close to one in a million, it may not be the only one that could do the job. Stephen's computer simulations have shown that the number of potential solutions to the problem of passing on information in living organisms is so huge that it is not easy to say whether ours is absolutely the only viable answer. His prediction is that if life exists on another planet, then we might see some similarities, but some of the specifics might be different. But what does this tell us about a creator – if it says anything at all?

In the end, Stephen has a lot of unanswered scientific questions, but that's the whole point of his job. Like any other field of human enquiry, science is driven forward by curiosity and wonder. The most important and interesting questions are often the most difficult to answer, but they are also the most fulfilling – and every new answer raises even more questions.

Stephen's queries about the genetic code also raise a number of philosophical or theological questions. Why does life exist? What is it for? For most people, these are far more important than the scientific questions. DNA research can help cure diseases, but it cannot tell us why we are here.

Stephen is not looking for scientific arguments for God, but he is interested in the meaning of things as well as the mechanisms. His scientific research is complementary to his theological thoughts and questions, providing fuel for the discussion and lighting up new questions in his mind. What he sees of the fruitful universe is compatible with his belief in a God who wanted to create life.

Before we come back to these deeper questions, the next chapter takes this conversation further, exploring the forces that keep things alive. The inner life of the cell thrives on the constant movement of molecules, but what keeps things moving in the right direction? We are facing the same questions: What's so special about life, why is it here, and where is it heading?

Chapter 4

Artistic Molecules: How messy processes form ordered life

At close range, Monet's paintings can look like random collections of different-coloured blobs of paint. You might be tempted to think they were the work of a child, not someone who had studied painting for many years. In fact, the word "impressionism" was coined by a critic to insult what he thought was a terrible new form of art.

Monet's painting *Impression, Sunrise* is the one that inspired the name "impressionist". It wasn't the first painting of this type, and Monet certainly wasn't the only artist trying the technique at the time, but perhaps it was one of the most striking examples. Seen up close, the whole thing looks like a mess of grey streaks. Nothing seems beautiful, and it doesn't make a lot of sense. I can see how an art critic looking for a more traditional kind of beauty could have been offended.

When we look at the whole canvas from a distance, however, the meaning of the blobs emerges. The overall order and beauty of the scene is suddenly revealed, and we can clearly see the boats and the reflection of the sun on the water. There is an impression of movement and the twinkling of sunlight. In the sun's reflection on the rippling waves, it's almost as if bright spots are sparkling in constant random motion.

Impressionist paintings only make sense from a distance, when their touches of light and colour blend together into a seamless whole. Standing back from the canvas, something wonderful takes shape. It took a while to catch on, but art galleries today are full of people standing far away from French impressionist paintings (sometimes a bit too far if there are too many people around), enjoying the beauty of rural landscapes or people at work or play.

This idea of order from randomness is important scientifically. We are about to explore the ways in which randomness contributes to the fruitfulness of the living world, but what does that mean for faith? When God created something from nothing, how was randomness part of what was declared "very good"? To see how these ideas fit together, we need to focus again on the inner world of the cell.

Like Monet's paintings, the inside of a living organism is a place where randomness at one level can result in order on a higher level. Close up, the molecules in a cell are bouncing around in all directions, but on a larger scale these movements are actually producing useful structures and patterns. When Monet painted, he may not have given a huge amount of thought to the position of every single dab of colour, but there was a lot of intention in the overall effect. In a similar way, molecules are moving without thought – randomly bumping into each other – but the overall effect is that of a living cell.

The ultimate question here is, "What is life?", and the random behaviour of molecules is at least part of the answer. One of the people who wants to understand how this happens is Dr Rhoda Hawkins, a physicist from the University of Sheffield who uses mathematics and computers to understand how cells move.

As a student studying mouse stem cells, I (Ruth) accidentally made beating heart cells and gave myself a fright when I saw them down a microscope for the first time. In the eighteenth-century the Scottish botanist Robert Brown may have had a similar scare when he peered down a microscope at pollen grains in water and saw them jiggling around. The movement itself was nothing to do with being alive, because particles of soot or metal dust moved around in exactly the same way, but no one in Brown's day could understand why it was happening.

Seventy-five years later, Einstein came up with a theory that explained what has come to be known as "Brownian motion". Like the flickering of sunlight on waves, the molecules in a glass of water are in constant motion. On average, all the molecules end up roughly where they started, so the water looks completely stationary. When several water molecules bump into a pollen grain at the same time and in the same direction, they give it a kick that moves it along. A little drop of water contains so many molecules that this happens fairly often, and the pollen looks like it's jiggling around spontaneously. This sort of random movement is happening all the time in a living cell, and it turns out to be very useful.

If you watched an impressionist paint a picture, you might be unable to predict where the next splash of colour was going to be placed, but after a while you would probably be able to tell what the overall picture was going to be. In a similar way, randomly moving molecules can be useful because they develop an average behaviour that is entirely predictable. None of us could predict the roll of a single die, but if I threw a handful of dice thousands of times I would probably get a six about one-sixth of the time. So in science, "random" isn't a negative word as it so often is in everyday life. Instead of meaning purposeless or pointless, it just means that individual events are unpredictable – while on a larger scale the overall effect might be entirely predictable.

When lots of molecules get together, a pattern emerges that is related to the character of the individual parts. To stick with the example of water, it has some unique properties:

- It fills the gaps in porous materials, making them wet.

- It boils at a much higher temperature than other molecules of a similar size.

- Insects can walk over its surface.

- Its frozen form floats on its liquid form.

Some of these properties are very useful, and they come from the way individual H_2O molecules interact with each other. They stick together, making water wet and hard to boil. Most interestingly for children, when water freezes it forms organized crystals that are much less dense than liquid water, so they can form ice on a lake or be made into snowballs and snowmen. The molecules of living things are more complex than water, so when they get together they can develop properties that are even more useful.

What if an artist invented a process where the pictures painted themselves? If dots of paint jiggled themselves around until they formed a picture, would that still be art? The cell is like a self-painting picture, where the molecules move around to form structures that keep it alive.

For example, every cell in your body is surrounded by a specialized kind of fat called phospholipid. At one end of each molecule is a "head" that likes water and the other end is a "tail" that hates it. When phospholipid molecules are dropped into water, they line up together with their tails in the air, or circle round to form droplets with their tails on the inside. They can also make double layers, surrounding a pocket of water.

The outer membrane of every cell is one of these "lipid bilayers". The phospholipid molecules are constantly moving around, but overall it stays intact. (Other protective layers stop the cells being damaged or drying out, so the overall effect can be a tough body that contains a lot of water.) This process of molecules coming together to form new structures is called self-assembly.

Self-assembly doesn't just keep a cell intact; it also helps it to move around. Inside each cell, individual molecules of a protein called actin jiggle around and bump into each other, sticking together to form long flexible strands thousands of subunits long. These filaments form the cell's internal skeleton, and they can assemble, dissemble, and reassemble again in beautifully coordinated ways that change the cell's shape or move it around.

Actin filaments can travel along a bit like a conveyer belt or caterpillar track (see figure 4, page 107). Instead of travelling back in a circle, the subunits drop off one end and join on to the other. The overall effect is that the filament moves along by growing in one direction and shrinking behind. Again, the random movement of molecules on a very tiny scale has contributed to a useful result on a larger scale – but how can that move a whole cell? In this case, there is some extra energy involved.

When Rhoda first started to look at whole cells, she asked the sorts of questions a biologist wouldn't usually consider. Why can a rock or the water in a pool only start moving if something pushes it, while a typical cell – which looks like a microscopic blob of jelly – can move around independently?

You don't have to look far to find videos of single cells moving around, or squeezing through narrow gaps to catch bacteria. When Rhoda saw these films she was so intrigued that cell movement became the main focus of her research. Organisms are made of exactly the same chemical elements as everything else, and they obey the same laws of physics and chemistry, so what is it that makes them alive? At least part of the answer is to do with balance.

A drop of ink will spread out in water until the two are completely blended together. This is the same for any non-living thing – its molecules go with the flow until they eventually reach a balanced state when things are no longer changing. When a new force comes into play, things are pushed out of balance until they settle again.

Non-living things are like sailing boats that just sit still and float around in whichever direction the wind pushes them. When the wind dies down, they stay in a balanced state until another gust comes along. For example, a rock doesn't move by itself, but it can be ground down by wind and weather, and washed away by a stream. Those particles of rock could settle in the sea and eventually form sedimentary rock, but if that rock is near a geological fault line it may be pushed upward and the process begins all over again.

Cells are more like steam ships that can drive themselves forward, overcoming the friction of the water and accelerating on to the right destination. They resist the tendency to relax by taking on board nutrients to fuel their internal generators. This energy drives their inner processes forward, keeping them active and ordered. When the energy supplies run out, the process runs out of steam fairly quickly and the cell begins to decay. A return to a balanced state involves no movement, no order in its molecules, and, in the end, no life.

One of the ways in which scientists can try to understand what life is by attempting to copy it. For example, a group of researchers in the US came up with metal rods that are about the same size and can move around at about the same speed as a bacterium. One end of each rod is made of platinum, and the other is gold. When the rods are put in a solution of hydrogen peroxide, the platinum end stimulates a chemical reaction, which creates a flow or current in the solution, pushing the rod forward.

These "nanomotors" are extremely simple compared with a living cell, but they're a start. A number of other people have tried the same thing, and their efforts are gradually getting more sophisticated. We are only just beginning to understand living things, but appreciating how complex they are is one of the first steps.

The other thing that amazes people like Rhoda is the ability of living things to interact. Individual molecules can self-assemble in certain ways, but when they have their own energy source they can interact in new ways and move independently, as if they have a mind of their own. Metal rods could be made to interact with magnets, but those forces would affect each rod in exactly the same way – and would give nothing like the complexity of movement that comes from biological systems.

One of the most fascinating sights I have seen on a winter evening are the huge flocks of starlings that wheel around as they come in to roost. Many thousands of birds can fly together in a single, huge group known as a murmuration, and each time the flock changes direction it pulsates and changes shape in weirdly synchronized ways. It's as if an impressionist painting had come to life.

These flocking behaviours arise spontaneously when large numbers of animals come together. Each bird is self-propelled, but a collective behaviour emerges. Flying close together helps the birds to avoid predators as they come in to their roosting site. As they fly, they steer in an average direction. Whenever they change direction, they have to avoid crashing into each other – so they may need to change the formation they're flying in. When these three rules are programmed into a computer, the same wonderfully organic-looking process is produced. On a much smaller scale, a similar process is happening to a group of molecules inside a cell when it moves.

If an entire flock of birds were captured in a very fine, light net, they might keep on moving by pushing on the inside of the net to change its shape and position. In a similar way, a cell moves when its internal skeleton pushes against its outer membrane. Like starlings coming in to land, the molecules inside that cell are constantly moving, but there is an overall pattern to the movement. Random motion brings the subunits together, but energy helps the filaments to form in a certain way and keeps them moving along. The subunits of each filament are constantly moving as more and more subunits are dropping off one end and being added to the other, pushing against the outer membrane of the cell.

The cell's inner skeleton can also help a whole body to move. In cells, cargo is fetched and carried by specialist motor proteins that grip onto the actin filaments with what look like feet. These "feet" can step along the filament by letting go, swinging round and sticking on further up. By repeating this cycle over and over again, these delivery service proteins can walk along the filament, using it as a pathway to carry cargo around the cell, burning up chemical energy to fuel the movement (see figure 5, page 108).

Muscles use similar motor proteins in groups with multiple feet. Actin filaments have a direction for travel, like lanes in a motorway. If one of these motor protein groups has its feet on two different filaments, the feet end up walking in opposite directions and pulling the filaments closer together. One protein can only exert a small force, but with thousands of actin filaments and motors together inside a muscle cell, this squeezing effect is multiplied many times (see figure 6, page 108). When thousands of muscle cells are joined together, the overall effect can be strong enough to lift heavy weights.

In the same way that order and meaning emerge from dots of paint when they are arranged in the right way, coordinated cell movement emerges from the self-assembly of molecules, with an injection of chemical energy. The cell is tugged along by the combined effort of filaments pushing at the front of the cell and motor proteins heaving away at the back.

The same mechanisms can make a cell change shape and squeeze through small spaces. If the gap is very tiny the cell's nucleus can also change shape, and this is one of the things Rhoda is researching.

In a sense, Rhoda's work is a bridge between the small and large scales, looking at the properties that emerge when atoms and molecules get together in the form of living organisms. Working at the cellular level produces a beauty of its own kind; many biologists enjoy collecting stunning pictures from their work with microscopes and display them in their presentations. Rhoda collaborates very closely with these people, and gets to appreciate their work as well as her own more mathematical representations of cells.

For Rhoda, it is a huge privilege to be able to work on these intricate and fascinating mechanisms, understanding why such insignificant-looking blobs of jelly can move around on their own.

The really big question is, how far does this research go toward explaining the unique properties of living things?

To begin with, it is now a little easier to define what life is. The standard definition usually includes taking in nutrients, responding to external signals, adapting to the environment, growth, and reproduction. We can also say that living organisms consume energy to maintain a complex combination of order and disorder, and that random processes can produce fruitful interactions.

There is also the question of how life arose in the first place. It's a long jump from an individual self-assembly process to a whole cell, but scientists believe that interactions like these may have been involved in the origin of life on earth (page 24).

The more we find out about how living things work, the less "mystery" there is – less of the ignorant or superstitious type of wonder. On the other hand, there is a greater sense of mystery, wonder, and excitement at the complexity of things: the beautifully coordinated mechanisms and clever solutions. There is also excitement at the questions that remain unanswered, and that is what drives science forward.

Using the tools of physics to study living things will always be a challenge, but the task of a scientist has always been to ask difficult questions and to try to find answers to them. In the end, Rhoda hopes to contribute to our understanding of cell movement in the immune system and in cancer.

What about the theological questions? On a more personal level, Rhoda is interested in the ideas that come from seeing order emerging from disorder. It seems that God uses randomness as part of his creative processes in the living world, using random processes to create new types of order. What about on a human scale – does he have a final purpose that makes sense of details in our lives that don't seem to make sense to us at the time? There may be some answers to these questions, but they are not always completely clear – understanding them will always be an ongoing process, and the closing chapters explore them further.

Having learned how cells live and move, the next chapter is about the dance of the cells that produces a whole organism – a field of research that invites a completely different set of questions.

Chapter 5

Dance of the Cells:
Embryonic development

In just nine months, a single cell develops into a kicking, squealing baby. The most mysterious part of this process is the first few weeks, when it can seem as if nothing much is happening. Until a developing embryo has arms and legs it is hard to imagine it as an individual, but these are actually the most important stages of development, laying the foundation for everything that is to come. While the embryo is just a ball of cells, or a tiny jellybean-shaped mass, a huge amount of activity is going on – and it all starts with just one cell.

The human egg is about a tenth of a millimetre in diameter, and is packed full of nutrients, proteins, a metre of DNA (see Chapter 2), and all the ingredients it needs to start growing. The father's sperm then provides another metre of DNA, and the list is complete. Everything that's needed to start a unique life is right there in that fertilized egg.

The development of an embryo is like a dance, as cells form and fold themselves into the different organs of the body. Some dances are very tightly choreographed, but any dancer will tell you that choreography alone doesn't make a good show. The whole cast are constantly watching and responding to each other. Their skills, personalities, and physiques influence how they interpret the moves. The music guides them and gives an overall atmosphere to the piece, as do the costumes, stage, lighting, and set. The responses of the audience add some further fuel to the performance. All of these parts come together to create the whole experience, so every show is slightly different.

In a similar way, DNA provides all the recipes for making an animal, but they are not enough to determine what goes on. A host of other molecules and environmental cues are also involved, and there are always slight variations along the way. Development is not a completely predictable process, and it's not easily reduced to one set of factors or another. This is something that Jeff Hardin knows only too well.

When Jeff was a student, he caught sight of a sea-urchin embryo and was immediately hooked. He is now a professor at the University of Wisconsin-Madison in the USA, where he teaches cell and developmental biology. The main question he asks in his research is, how does a single cell develop into a complex organism? Jeff also finds himself asking philosophical or even theological questions about beauty, and the significance of the organisms that develop from such humble beginnings.

This chapter will look at our own development from the perspective of a dance, sharing the sense of wonder that so many scientists feel when they study these processes.

Warm-up: week 1 – fertilization to implantation

The opening act of the dance of development appears to be a very simple warm-up. A single fertilized egg divides in two, then four, eight, and so on. The ball becomes more compact, a hollow opens up in the centre, and after a week it implants in the wall of the womb.

Like a professional dance troupe, from the outside this tiny mass of cells looks as if it is moving serenely from one stage of the dance to another, but the story is very different on the inside. A ballerina dancing on pointe shoes is working incredibly hard, and so is a dividing cell. Just as the dancer's muscles are tensing and relaxing, the act of dividing in two is also achieved by the cell's internal skeleton. The DNA duplicates and slides to either end of the cell along tracks called microtubules. Long filaments of actin (see Chapter 4) also form inside the cell, elongating and nipping it in the middle until it is pinched in half.

The focus of Jeff's own research is the way that connections are made and broken between cells. In the same way that dancers might transition between working in pairs or groups, forming lines or scattering across the stage, one of the most important forces in embryonic development is the way that cells grab on to or let go of each other as they multiply and move around the body.

Jeff studies development in a tiny transparent worm called C. elegans, which shares many of the processes that shape our own bodies. As he often says to his students, you can learn a lot about a Mercedes from a Toyota. Driven by his love of the visual, Jeff and his team have invented some specialized microscopy techniques that allow them to monitor these embryos as they grow over time.

For example, the process of compacting into a ball begins when neighbouring cells form connections between each other. The outer cells make "tight junctions", which are held together by proteins that stick out from the surface of each cell and interlock to form an impenetrable barrier. The cells on the inside of the ball then make "gap junctions" with each other, which are like tiny pipes that allow small molecules to be shared between cells. These connections help the ball of dividing cells to take a more complex shape later on.

Orientation: weeks one to three – fertilization to early embryo

Any group of dancers has to orient themselves properly while they rehearse for a performance. Where will the audience sit, and how far away are they? Where are the wings, and which places are out of sight? In a similar way, before a cluster of dividing cells can even begin to look like a proper organism, it has to find its bearings. It has to identify which will be the head end and which will be the rump; which is left and right, front and back.

The first sign of this dimensionality in the clump of cells is when it squeezes into a tight ball. The cells on the outside go on to form the placenta and embryonic membranes, and the inner cells become the embryo itself. The non-embryonic tissues develop first, so at the moment scientists think these determine how the dimensions of the embryo are laid out. There are clues, from studying other animals, that the place where the sperm enters the egg may also play a role in this process.

The embryo starts to develop in a symmetrical way, but later that symmetry is broken. For example, most adult animals appear to be a mirror image from left to right, but things are very different on the inside. In your own body you probably have your heart slightly to one side, two lobes in one lung and three in the other, and differences in your liver, gut, and other organs.

Body asymmetry is caused by a cluster of cells that develop at one end of the embryo when it is around three weeks old. These cells establish subtle differences on the left side of the body that ultimately give the left and right sides of the body their distinctive characteristics. If these cells are damaged or fail to function properly, the individual can develop *situs inversus solitus*, where the organs are a complete mirror image of the normal pattern. This is a harmless condition that happens in about one in 10,000 people,[6] but if the organs are a partial mirror image, this can cause severe problems or even fatality.

Taking on roles: week one to adulthood

One more thing has to happen before a dance performance can go ahead: each of the dancers has to be assigned their own role or character. This may involve some differences in the choreography for each person or group of people, as well as acting skills and perhaps some unique costumes. In a similar way, the cells in an embryo must also take on their own specific roles.

In the very early stages of development, every cell has the potential to form any of the tissues of the embryo, placenta, or surrounding membranes. The first roles are assigned after the cells begin to pull into a tighter ball. Inside is a clump of cells which will form the embryo,[7] and these have the potential to become blood, muscle, skin, and all the other tissues of the adult body.

Taking on a specialized role involves long-term changes in a cell's structure and the kinds of molecules it produces. These alterations affect what the cell can do, as well as the way it looks. The driving

---

6   This has nothing to do with being left-handed, which is to do with the
     activity of the brain – not the structure of the body.
7   Embryonic stem cells are derived from these tissues.

forces behind this process are the chemical signals which switch genes on or off, so they can start or stop making certain proteins. Once a cell is committed to its fate, there is no easy way of going back.

As skin cells develop, they flatten out and produce lots of tough keratin. Skin grows from the bottom up, as multiple protective layers over the whole body. The older, dead cells are constantly brushed off against our clothes and any objects we come into contact with.

Red blood cells become flat and disc-shaped and start making haemoglobin, which carries oxygen around the body. They even break down their DNA allowing them to fit in as much of this useful molecule as possible. Once their DNA is removed, red blood cells can no longer multiply, so they survive little more than a hundred days in the bloodstream before they wear out and are recycled.

Nerve cells are extremely long and thin, and can transmit an electrical signal from one part of the body to another. Some nerves can be a metre or more in length, reaching all the way from the base of your spine to your toes. Similar to electrical wires, these cells are supported and insulated by specialized fatty cells that wrap themselves around the outside. Like red blood cells, nerves cannot divide any more but they can sometimes regrow if they are damaged.

Forming and folding: week three

Once a dance group has warmed up, found their bearings, and roles have been assigned, the performance can really begin. For an embryo, the dance begins in earnest with a period of forming and folding that happens in week three. This phase of development is driven by the movement of different cell types as they go on multiplying, sticking together, and letting go. At different points in the dance the cells change shape, form sheets, slide past each other, or spread out across surfaces.

In the same way that cells divide in the warm-up phase (page 36), one of the main techniques a cell can use to change its shape is by mobilizing its inner skeleton. The filaments of the skeleton are anchored to the outer membrane and can also be connected to grippy "feet" which stick to surfaces. By growing, shrinking or moving in certain directions, the filaments can stretch, squeeze, or crawl the cell forward in the right direction (see Chapter 4).

Jeff and his team are especially interested in the molecules that anchor cells together. Jutting out of the cell's membrane, these proteins can act like Velcro. So if a few cells in a connected sheet contract, they can affect the shape of the whole embryo.

Making a complicated-looking origami model might seem difficult, but all you need is a series of instructions about how to fold and turn the paper. The embryo develops in a similar way, because each of the cells has its own instructions about which part of the body it is in, what signals to respond to, or where to move next. Some people speak of life unfolding, but actually it folds up. By following these instructions, the embryo pleats, pinches, and tucks itself, so that over a period of many weeks it will eventually take on the basic shape and features we recognize in a baby.

Toward the end of week two, the implanted mass of tissues contains two fluid-filled cavities, each lined with a layer of cells. In week three, the embryo then begins to develop in the place where these two layers of cells meet. First, a thickened ridge takes shape along the top layer of cells, with a bump at one end that will become the head. Some of the cells then detach from the top layer and crawl down through the ridge, creating a middle layer that will become the core muscles, bones, and organs of the future child. The ridge then deepens and closes over to produce a space where the spinal cord will develop (see figure 7, page 109). As these cell movements happen, the whole embryo also elongates and curls up.

Making patterns: week three to adolescence

As a dance show goes on, the performers may take on more defined roles, breaking from larger groups into pairs or individual soloists. These new roles allow the dancers to make even more complex figures and patterns in the dance as it comes to its climax, and the same happens in the dance of the cells.

As development progresses and becomes more complex, the role of each cell must become more precisely defined. The instructions for these changes come from within the cells themselves, as they give and receive chemical signals. These signals and the changes they initiate build up more detail, like a picture coming into focus as more pixels are defined.

One of the most striking examples of body patterning is when each section of the embryo is given its own unique character, from head to rump. The whole process is controlled by a family of genes called Hox. These genes produce proteins that clamp on to the DNA in different places, activating a whole collection of other genes.

As an embryo goes through the forming and folding process, its Hox genes are switched on one by one. A wave of signalling passes down the body, identifying each segment as it goes. The identity of a segment tells it which organs to make, so this very early phase – when the embryo looks a bit like a peanut – is one of the most important stages in its development.

The Hox genes are beautiful because of the way they are organized. They are in several clusters on four different chromosomes. As the embryo develops, the cells at the head end activate the first genes in the Hox clusters, giving that section of the body its unique identity. Then the cells just below the head switch on the second set of genes in the cluster, and so on. A wave of gene activation passes down the embryo, specifying each section of the trunk in turn.[8] The order of the genes in each cluster is the same as the order in which they first appear in the body – both in time and space.

This kind of genetic arrangement is completely unique. No other cluster of genes has been found to be arranged this way, so it is one of the great wonders of developmental biology. Every animal that scientists have studied so far shares this same system of body patterning. There are some differences between animals, with increasing levels of complexity from worms and insects through to humans. It's interesting to compare the pattern of Hox genes between different animals, as well as the DNA code of the genes themselves, and the effect these differences have during development. This is the science of evolutionary and developmental biology, or "evo-devo" as it's often called, and it is one of the newest and most exciting sources of evidence for the evolution of all animals from a common ancestor.

---

8   Once a Hox gene is switched on it can stay switched on in the next few
     sections of cells, so the activation of the genes is somewhat overlapping.

The climax of the dance: weeks four to nine

In some dance performances, things may be a little unclear at first, until we begin to realize who each of the characters represents and what they are doing. As the story goes on, things start to make even more sense and a definite narrative takes shape.

As the dance of the cells reaches its climax, recognizable structures begin to appear: a head, eyes, nose, ears, limbs, hands, and feet. Each organ is formed by the same processes that have already been described: cells change shape or size, make and break connections, crawl from place to place, and multiply in different areas at different rates.

The hand is a wonderful example of how organs are formed. First, a patch of cells multiplies rapidly to make a bud-shaped bump on one side of the body. Patterns of signalling proteins switch genes on or off to specify one end of this new limb from the other, top and bottom, left and right. As the bud grows longer, a paddle-shaped hand develops at the end. The dividing cells start to take on specific roles: skin, cartilage, bone, muscle, and tendons. Blood vessels keep pace with the growth, supplying oxygen and nutrients to all the cells. Nerve cells migrate from the spine into each limb, connecting hand to brain. Finally, the webbed flap of skin between each digit disappears, revealing tiny fingers.

On a very large stage with an orchestra pit, the dancers who are close to the front of the stage might find it easier to respond to the music than those who are at the very back. In a similar way, the signals involved in body patterning sometimes diffuse outward from a single location. The cells closer to the source of the signal can develop differently from the ones that are further away.

In the developing hand, a signalling protein is produced by a collection of cells on the side that forms the thumb. This signal diffuses across the hand, activating a unique cascade of genes (including some of the Hox genes) that gives each finger its own identity. So each finger receives its identity from the webbed flaps of tissue that link them together, not the finger cells themselves. Much of what we know about limb development comes from research on chickens and mice, because our arms develop in a similar way and we share many of the same genes.

Reducing the cast: week two to adulthood

In most ballets, there will be some acts where one or two of the dancers take centre stage for a solo. Or perhaps a small group may break away to express something different from the rest of the cast. At these times, some of the people involved may be hiding in the wings, reducing the amount of distraction on the stage so the audience can focus on the solo. In a tragedy, the cast may be reduced as one character after another makes their final bow.

In a similar way, about half of a baby's cells – including around two-thirds of its nerve cells – have to leave the dance before it is born. The disappearance of the webbed skin of the developing hand is a classic example of this process. Another quite dramatic example comes from the nervous system. The growing ends of nerve cells migrate outward into the developing brain, limbs, and other organs. A nerve must reach its target and connect with another cell, or it will often die and be broken down and recycled.

For a cell, this programmed curl-up-and-die process is more like fireworks than a funeral. It starts when the compartment containing the DNA shrinks and breaks into pieces. The main body of the cell then appears to boil as parts of it begin to break away. In the end, all the fragments are swallowed up by specialized cleaning cells.

The default strategy for most cells seems to be self-destruction, and the only way they can survive is to form connections with other cells. For example, a nerve cell migrating out from an embryo's spinal cord must connect with a muscle so it can receive "survival factors" that help it avoid self-destruction.

The same mechanisms are also in place in adult bodies. Cells must connect or die, which is useful in limiting abnormal behaviour that might lead to cancer. Cells that have been damaged also die in this way, and infected cells receive signals from the immune system that tell them to self-destruct.

After all the sculpting and shaping in weeks three to nine, the embryo has begun to look like a small person – though perhaps a slightly alien-looking one. Most of what remains to be done before birth is simply growth in the right directions.

The metaphor of the dance of the cells emerged very naturally while this chapter was being written, inspired by Jeff's own way of seeing the processes of development. The dynamic movements and interactions of trillions of cells come together in a complex, ever-changing, and multiplying arrangement to form a fully functioning organism.

Jeff's sense of curiosity and wonder is one of the main drivers behind his work. He feels enormously privileged to be able to understand the intricate processes of embryonic development. He also believes that one of his roles as a scientist is to take time to appreciate the things he studies for their own sake, and not just their usefulness in helping to improve medical treatments.

As someone who originally went to university to study music and physics, before finally being hooked by biology, Jeff is in a good place to appreciate the aesthetic aspects of his work. He believes there is something about the beauty of living things that is valuable for their own sake, which cannot be reduced to scientific explanations alone.

As well as his qualifications in biology, Jeff has also studied theology, and he is the only scientist at his university who is involved in the religious studies programme. So when he teaches developmental biology, Jeff always starts by quoting some ancient poetry from the Hebrew Scriptures:

> For you created my inmost being; you knit me together in my mother's womb. I praise you because I am fearfully and wonderfully made; your works are wonderful, I know that full well. My frame was not hidden from you when I was made in the secret place, when I was woven together in the depths of the earth. Your eyes saw my unformed body...
> **Psalm 139:13–16 (NIV)**

He goes on to say that although the writer knew very little about development, he clearly appreciated how wonderful it is. Jeff's goal is to help his students learn to enjoy the intricate processes that go into forming an embryo, whatever their beliefs might be.

Moving from embryos and zooming out to the bigger picture, the next question is, what caused living things to form this way in the first place? Are the processes of life heading along any particular routes? This is a question that the palaeobiologist Simon Conway Morris has been asking throughout his career.

Chapter 6

The Map of Life: Is evolution compatible with purpose?

We all get lost at times in our lives. Whether it is as a child on a family day out or as an adult on a hike, we have all known that sinking feeling when we realize we have no idea where we are or where to go next. If the paths are well marked it may be easier to navigate our way out, or find the people we are supposed to be with. If the track is faint, we might be in a little more trouble than we had expected. Of course, with a map, we could be a little more oriented – as long as we know how to use it. On the other hand, some people quite like getting lost and are happy to ramble about exploring the different routes, as long as they get to a useful destination in the end.

Other creatures in the living world make our attempts at navigating look pathetic. Migrating birds can take themselves from one country to another, sometimes travelling halfway across the globe to find somewhere to breed or escape extreme weather. Red knots are among the most widely travelled birds, flying up to 15,000 kilometres between their winter and summer homes. There are always some that get lost or are blown off course, but the general accuracy of these vast journeys is impressive. Different birds can find their way using the sun, stars, or magnetic fields. Their ancestors have been making these journeys for millennia, so in a sense they are also following well-worn paths.

Some journeys in the living world happen in time rather than space. A population of organisms may find itself in a habitat where it can live, grow, and multiply. The place might be adequate but far from perfect, so anything that helps these creatures to adapt to their environment (see page 24, Chapter 3) will help them to thrive even more. As the generations go by, genetic changes accumulate and affect the way that population interacts with its surroundings. Over a very long period of time, they may find themselves in the same location, but relating to their environment in a different way. What if those processes of change were also following a series of pathways – a map of life? How does that fit in with our own ideas of a purpose for the world, or even the existence of a creator?

The concept of the map of life has its origins in an event that took place 500 million years ago, when an underwater mudslide engulfed a collection of organisms that would look extremely strange by today's standards. Some had five eyes and a toothed trunk, while others had a square mouth and oddly shaped legs – or perhaps they were fins? By comparison, dinosaurs are somewhat tame and forgettable. Here were some of the most fantastic creatures that have ever walked, swum, or slithered on earth.

These mud-covered animals became fossilized and, through the movement of the earth's tectonic plates, became part of the great mountain range that we now call the Canadian Rockies. In 1909, an American geologist named Charles Doolittle Walcott went on an expedition to this spot and was amazed to find the fossils of soft-bodied animals. Normally the softer parts of an organism decompose before they can fossilize, so this was a very rare find. Walcott named the site the "Burgess Shale" and began to collect as many specimens as possible. This was one of the landmark discoveries of biology. In the same way that the Galapagos Islands are historic for evolutionary biologists, the Burgess Shale is now a significant place for palaeontologists.

Most of the 65,000 fossils that Walcott and his team dug up were stored away in the archives of the Smithsonian Museum in Washington, DC. As secretary of the museum, he was too busy to study them for long, and when he died they were left to gather dust.

Decades later, a group of Canadian and British scientists returned to the Burgess Shale. At the same time, a young student happened to see some of Walcott's fossils in a class at Bristol University and they sparked his interest. He got in touch with Harry Whittington, the leader of the Burgess Shale project in Cambridge, and won a place as a research student in his lab.

The young student was Simon Conway Morris, and he spent the next three years painstakingly removing layers of rock from small animal fossils, photographing, and drawing them. The work was repetitive but hugely rewarding, because most of the creatures he was revealing with his micro-hammer were previously unknown to science. Now that he is a professor at Cambridge University, Simon sees these fossils as a sign that life is more than just a chaotic jumble of organisms struggling to survive. There may well be a pattern to what is going on in the living world – a network of paths for the journey through time.

If the whole of earth's 4.6-billion-year history is reduced to the scale of a human arm span, the first fossil evidence of bacterial life doesn't appear until around the right armpit. By the left armpit we have evidence for complex cells, and multicellular life around the left elbow. By the left wrist we have the first evidence of recognizable animals – the fossils found in the Burgess Shale. After this came a massive explosion of diversity. Humans appeared around 200,000 years ago – on the very tip of the fingernails. (Note: this timescale is approximate because our knowledge in this area is growing rapidly, and in some instances scientists' opinions vary.)

Let's take a walk through ancient seas to find out what some of the Burgess Shale animals may have been like when they were alive. *Wiwaxia* is definitely something you wouldn't want to stand on at the beach. At about two and a half to five centimetres long, its top is covered in tough scales, a double row of which stick up like knives. Underneath is a soft, snail-like body with a rasping mouth for feeding off the sea floor.

At just under ten centimetres long, *Opabinia* is one of the larger animals in the sea. Its shell is jointed like a lobster's, but it also has a series of flaps down the side of its body that could be used for propelling itself through the water – or perhaps along the ground? Its most distinctive features are a cluster of five protruding eyes, and a long nozzle ending in a clawed tip and armoured mouth.

Hallucigenia is another one to handle carefully. It might be a centimetre or so smaller than *Wiwaxia*, but it has two rows of very sharp pointed spines along its back. Underneath are two rows of tentacles for walking on, each of which has a pair of claws at the end. It took a while for scientists to identify which is the head and which is the tail end of this animal, but we now know that the thinner end sticking out from its body is its neck and head.

The largest of the Burgess Shale animals is around a metre long. *Anomalocaris* also has a lobster-like body with flaps sticking out down the sides. Two jointed forelimbs are probably used to shovel food into its mouth, where they meet its fearsome square jaw with four sets of pointed teeth.

Other animals sit, scurry, swim or dig around on the sea floor, including different kinds of trilobites, worms, and sponges. There are also creatures that look a little like eels, corals, and sea anemones. Together, these weird and wonderful animals provide a clue to what the map of life might be like.

If you dropped a group of people off in the middle of a wood and left them to go for a walk, they would probably meander along the paths in different directions. If the paths were well designed, they could wander to their heart's content and all end up at the visitors' centre in time for tea. There they might find a map that showed them where they had been, outlining all the paths that converged on the tea room.

In the early days of his Burgess Shale research, Simon thought he was seeing animal forms that hadn't survived at all to the present day. This made some of his colleagues wonder whether the processes of evolution were more like a group of people setting off across a trackless waste, instead of a series of organized paths. One or two of them might make it to the café, but as there was no way of communicating this location to the others, the rest would probably just stay lost.

As more complete versions of the Burgess fossils were found, Simon's ideas became a little clearer. Many of these animals actually looked like primitive versions of ones that are alive today. For example, *Hallucigenia* is similar to velvet worms, *Anomalocaris* and *Opabinia* are similar to arthropods (the group of animals that includes insects, spiders, and crustaceans), and *Wiwaxia* could be a kind of mollusc or a relative of bristle worms.

In the same way that the well-worn paths in a woodland might converge on the visitors' centre, the routes that evolving populations are following often reach similar solutions to the challenges of life on earth – in a process called convergent evolution. For example, powered flight has evolved at least four times, and echolocation (using sound to "see" objects) six or seven times. The same enzymes have evolved over and over again, as has agricultural behaviour (for example, there are ants that farm fungi). So the map of life is a series of paths that evolving populations take through evolutionary time as they converge on the same solutions to the challenges of life on earth, time and time again.

The eye is one of the best examples of evolutionary processes reaching the same destination. Our own eyes operate like cameras, with a pupil to let in the right amount of light, a lens for focusing, and a retina for detecting the picture. At least seven other types of animal have this kind of eye, but the last common ancestor of any of these creatures did not. So the camera eye has evolved not once, but at least eight times.

Another famous example of convergent evolution comes from comparing the marsupial (pouched) and placental mammals. When Western scientists began to explore South America, they found a whole range of marsupials, either as fossils or live animals. These were named after the placental mammals they looked like: anteaters, cats, wolves, mice, moles, flying squirrels, and so on.

At first glance, the marsupial and placental sabre-toothed cats look like first cousins, but their last common ancestor (before South America was isolated from Africa by continental drift) was probably some kind of small, tree-climbing animal like an opossum or a tree shrew. Over the millennia, that animal's descendants came to live on two different land masses, where they evolved two different ways of having young – and also a range of different survival methods. On each continent, some of that shrew's descendants emerged into a way of life that involved being a large and very fearsome cat. So there may be some well-worn trails in the map of life, but the question is, how did those pathways get there in the first place?

Anyone walking through a forest might be tempted to stray off the path a little. They might be looking for a good photo opportunity, following a rare bird, or searching for the ideal spot for a picnic. In a dense and wild forest, those options might be less tempting. Wet feet, the danger of getting lost, or prickly plants might deter them from straying too far.

The constraints in the map of life are often also physical barriers. If you want to fly or glide through the air, you have to work with the force of gravity. If you want to swim, you have to push against the water. The paths are defined by the physical properties of the universe, and other limits on what can survive and flourish in different environments. Evolving populations cannot deviate from these established routes because other solutions are physically impossible. We can't just decide to fly off a cliff without a parachute or swim through quicksand. Any organism that is unable to work with the resources available to them will reach a literal dead end. Within these constraints, though, amazing things are possible.

Most ancient cathedrals have been modified over the centuries. Their various parts have to work together, so the nave may not be as long as some would like, but at least the choir can be heard everywhere in the building. Some things would have been nice but were too expensive to be realistic, like covering the entire ceiling with gold leaf. In among the compromises and the remnants of past projects, some aspects of the building – perhaps the acoustics or the overall visual effect – seem to have just about reached perfection.

In a similar way, evolution builds on what is available. Living organisms are full of historical constraints, compromises, and remnants of structures that are no longer needed. They are also limited by what is physically possible at the time. Some parts, though, seem close to perfect. The cells in the retina of your eye can detect a single photon of light, and a frog's nasal neurons can smell a single molecule. Under the right conditions, the mammalian ear is so sensitive that it can detect sounds only a little louder than air molecules banging against the eardrum (known as thermal noise). These systems have reached the limit of what is possible in a biological organism. The processes of evolution have navigated the map of life so successfully that, unless conditions change, there is no need to go anywhere else.

The concept of convergence has always been part of evolutionary theory, but Simon is one of the few scientists to have made it the focus of their research and begun to think about its deeper implications. One question he is interested in now is whether the limits that keep evolutionary processes on certain paths can be brought together as a set of organizing principles for biology.

In the same way that there is a periodic table for chemistry and a set of laws in physics, is there a deeper structure or pattern in biology that can be described in a relatively straightforward way? This is a question that biologists have been asking for a long time, but convergent evolution may be a hint in the right direction. In a sense, we are looking for the key to the map of life.

Living things, and the relationships between them, are far more complex than the atoms in a molecule or planets in a solar system. Any organizing principles for biology will probably be far more complex and harder to find than the physical laws or the periodic table. To help the search, Simon and his team have created an online database called mapoflife.org, which describes all the examples of convergent evolution that have been found so far.

One test of Simon's ideas would be if the history of life on earth were started again from the beginning. Would the outcome change just a little compared with what we see now, or very drastically? If evolution had headed off in a slightly different direction, perhaps today we would be avoiding Wiwaxia at the beach instead of sea urchins. Had the differences been fairly major, perhaps the most technically able species on earth would be living in the sea instead of on land.

The map of life ideally provides a clue as to what might happen in this (hopefully unlikely) scenario. If the programme of life were rerun, Simon thinks the outcome would be relatively similar to what we see today. The physical properties of the universe would remain the same, so the paths in the map of life would still be in the same place. There would probably be quite a few minor differences in the way things looked, and plenty of dead ends along the way, but the processes of evolution would almost certainly arrive at the same basic structures. But there are less destructive ways to test this idea than wiping out life on earth entirely.

At the moment it seems unlikely that we will ever find anything other than microbes on the other planets and moons in our own solar system, and a planet containing more complex life may be too far away for us to investigate it properly. But what if we could? Like Stephen Freeland (see Chapter 3), the greatest test of Simon's ideas would be if we found organisms living elsewhere in the universe.

The laws of physics are the same throughout the universe. So on a roughly earth-sized planet with a gaseous atmosphere and a similar force of gravity, there would probably be legs for walking and wings for flying. Some creatures would have efficient camera eyes, ears would detect noises, and noses would sniff.

Most of the animals on earth that we consider intelligent have excellent vision, warm bodies, and a relatively small number of offspring. They have large brains that enable them to remember, learn, hunt efficiently, and use tools. Some of them even use language and music, take part in complex social relationships, and play.

We have turned out to be the most technologically capable species on earth. If there were complex life on another planet, the situation might be similar. Science fiction movies that depict "little green men" could be more realistic than we think, because the sorts of organisms capable of travelling to another place in the universe might have to be a bit like us.

So perhaps there is a landscape of eyes and ears, legs and wings just waiting to be discovered by the processes of evolution as they search out the best solutions to the challenges of living on earth. What, then, does this say about the deep structure of the universe? The science is still too young to say whether scientists will be able to develop a general theory of biology, but the prospects look hopeful.

In recent years, Simon has turned his attention to more specific ideas about convergent evolution, and the first is the question of intelligence. Scientists used to think that only humans, and perhaps apes, were really clever. Now we know that cetaceans (the group that includes dolphins and whales), elephants, and some birds also have a talent for learning, knowledge, and comprehension in a similar way to humans. There are even signs of this kind of intelligence in the octopus, reptiles, and insects. These seem to be other, and very significant, examples of convergent evolution.

Another important question is whether any of these other species we think of as intelligent are conscious of their intelligence. They may seem to know that they know something, but perhaps they are just showing off a complex behaviour without realizing the significance of what they're doing. If they do turn out to be conscious of it, where did that ability come from? In the same way that mathematics seems to reflect the fundamental properties of the universe, perhaps consciousness reflects some sort of universal principle of rationality.

One of the most important questions for Simon is how a supposedly meaningless process has produced beings like us who see meaning all around us. What is the purpose of the living world? The processes of evolution may be wandering at random, but that doesn't mean the paths are there for no reason. This is a fascinating area to discuss, because it points to questions that lie beyond science. Might there be some kind of organizing mind behind the physical properties of the universe?

We may eventually find a deeper scientific explanation for why things are the way they are, but that wouldn't take away the fact that what we see is compatible with the existence of a God who wanted to create life – including intelligent life. Science can tell us how things are, but ultimately it cannot say why they exist. We are left to figure out which worldview makes best sense of the data.

Going on from here, we can ask some more questions about the meaning and purpose of what we see in the living world. One convergent property that is worth looking at in more detail is the ability of living things to work together. Cooperation is one of the great driving forces of biology, so much so that we could ask, "Are we part of a great 'snuggle for existence'?"

Chapter 7

The Snuggle for Existence:
The power of cooperation

What bird would choose to incubate its fragile and temperature-sensitive egg in the middle of a blizzard? The only animals that manage to successfully bring their young into the world, on land, during the Antarctic winter are emperor penguins. The way these creatures handle the harsh weather is not just inspiring; it is also one of the best demonstrations of the snuggle for existence in the living world.

As summer fades away, emperor penguins trek inland to breed, forming colonies of up to 20,000 pairs. But these groups are not just for companionship; they are essential for survival. All penguin species pair up and share the duties of rearing their young, but emperors are different in one special way: the males work together.

After mating and laying their eggs, the females all hurry back to the sea for a two-month fishing trip, leaving their partners behind to play a very long game of keepy-uppy. Each male balances his mate's egg on his feet, protecting it from the elements in a feathered brood pouch. He will eat nothing until the worst of the winter is over, so as soon as temperatures begin to drop below minus forty degrees centigrade, he huddles together with the others to save calories.

The inside of a penguin huddle is so warm that scientists have suggested that the famous shuffling movement of birds from the inside to the outside of the pack, so they all take a turn in the storm, is actually to lose some heat. When he breaks free of the huddle, the male can cool off, eat some clean snow, and preen a little before heading back in to warm up. The result of this game is that emperors are the only penguin species that don't defend a patch of territory in a nesting site – so instead of competing, they seem to be cooperating.

Over the last few decades, biologists have become more aware of examples like this, where members of a species work together – or even with other species. This research is raising important questions: Is cooperation actually one of the main driving forces in the living world? Are we involved in a "snuggle" as well as a struggle for existence?[9] Taking that question even further, is there evidence of self-giving interactions in the living world – where the giver does not receive anything in return (altruism) – and what can we say about our own behaviour in that area?

Jeff Schloss is a biologist and philosopher who has been focusing on these questions throughout his career. He is fascinated by stories like the penguin's egg-warming marathon. He's also interested in the hints that there is more to our own behaviour than science alone can explain. When he started out in research, Jeff studied an example of cooperation that was already famous among biologists.

It took a hundred years for the scientific community to accept that lichen is a partnership between at least two different organisms. For a long time, these crusty-looking growths on rocks and trees were thought to be a kind of plant, but eventually scientists realized they were fungi with thousands of single-celled algae or cyanobacteria (sometimes both) living inside. Once the two- (or multiple-) organism hypothesis was accepted, the next question was whether these species are working together in an equal way or if the fungus is preying like a parasite on the algae trapped inside its body.

We now know that both partners in a lichen benefit from their relationship. The tough outer body of the fungus provides a secure home for the microbes, protecting them from drying out or being damaged by the sun. In return, the microbes make carbohydrates that help the fungus to survive. Working as a team, a lichen can endure the most extreme conditions. All it needs is a surface to grow on, clean air, and a little bit of water and warmth every now and then.

Jeff believes that cooperation is a creative force that can produce completely new outcomes in the living world, from microscopic

9   This metaphor is from *Super Cooperators: Altruism, Evolution, and Why We Need Each Other to Succeed* (Edinburgh: Canongate, 2011), page xvii, by Martin Nowak with Roger Highfield.

details through to whole societies. Once organisms start working together, the mutual benefits can build up in a kind of reverse arms race that often leads to complete dependency on each other. Working together like this helps individuals to survive and thrive, passing on their genes to the next generation. So although competition against each other is a huge part of the way species develop over time, cooperation may have an equally important role in the process.

Starting with the world of the very small, there is a partnership right inside the cells of every organism that's visible to the naked eye. Our cells are like the fungus in a lichen – they need to acquire energy so they can do their work in the body. The fuel comes not from algae, but from tiny energy factories called mitochondria, which used to live independently.

The theory goes that a large bacterium swallowed, or was invaded by, smaller ones. The small bacteria happened to be equipped to do something the larger one couldn't do, which was to make energy from certain chemicals. Some of that energy was passed to the large bacterium, and, as part of the process, the smaller ones found a safe place to live. Once this accidental relationship started, it was too convenient to stop. Eventually, both bacteria became so dependent on each other that they could not survive apart. The new and more complex kinds of cells which came out of this type of partnership have become the building blocks for every living thing more sophisticated than a bacterium, from plankton to blue whales.

Once these more complex cells were formed, they could team up and start working together. Slime mould cells forage about on their own, as long as there is plenty of food available, but as soon as they get hungry they start seeking each other out. Bunching together, they go on a strange gyrating journey to form long stalks with fruiting bodies at the end. Spores are released into the air, which might land in a place where there is more to eat.

Cells can become even more dependent on each other if they bring different abilities to the partnership. The Portuguese man-of-war is a collection of tiny organisms called zooids that get together to form a mass of stinging, feeding tissue with tentacles up to 46 metres long. Each zooid comes as one of four types: for defence, reproduction, feeding, or floating. In other organisms, from plankton to people, the different kinds of cells have become so tightly joined together and dependent on each other that they form a single body.

At the scale of whole organisms, many species reproduce by bringing male and female gametes (eggs and sperm) together. Without this cooperative process of mixing up the genes from two parents, we would all be clones. Sometimes the parents even cooperate to raise their offspring to adulthood.

Some species go much further than just pairing off. They form societies where completely novel behaviours can happen. The penguin males and their eggs are one example of this, but there are plenty more. One extreme example is the ant queen, who has a brief encounter with a male which provides her with all the sperm she'll ever need; from then on she does nothing but sit in the middle of her colony laying eggs for the others to look after. She can produce more than 150 million offspring in her lifetime, and each one will take on a specific role in the group.

Jeff and many of his colleagues believe that cooperation is a vital part of the living world, from the most basic life form to the most complex society. Relationships appear to have been at the heart of – or even driven – every major transition in the evolution of life. From molecules to cells; from simple to complex cells; from single cells to multicellular organisms; from asexual to sexual organisms; and from individuals to communities, cooperation seems to be one of the main drivers for developing complexity among living things.

The same sorts of partnerships and behaviours crop up throughout the living world, and are a wonderful example of convergent evolution (see Chapter 6). The transition from molecules to cells has taken place multiple times. Plant and animal cells both contain different sub-cellular energy factories. Groups of isolated cells have come together, making the important transition to becoming a multicellular organism at least twenty-five separate times. Examples of organisms working in pairs and societies are too common to count, and they often seem to have evolved independently.

There are five main ways of cooperating, which we could compare with our own behaviours (though other organisms will be doing them in a much less considered way, and not always for the same reasons!).

1. MUTUAL BENEFITS

Each partner in the team receives the waste products, or other easily shareable benefits, of the other's lifestyle. The relationship might have started accidentally but keeps going in the long term because it works well. A good example of this are the single-celled algae that live inside coral polyps (see page 69).

2. TIT-FOR-TAT

This is a conscious giving and receiving, paying favours back and forth. So a vampire bat feeds its baby after a hunting trip, but it might also feed the baby of an unsuccessful hunter from the same colony. This can only work for animals that can spot the ones who don't pay back favours.

3. REPUTATION

If I am seen being kind to you, then other people might be more likely to be kind to me. This also happens in other species. So a cleaner fish appears to earn a good reputation when a larger fish or other animal in need of a clean watches it pick parasites off another. And when our good deeds are less obvious, we need communication methods – like language – to pass on the word. Another way to communicate is by giving off unconscious signals. In one study, students could intuitively pick up if a stranger was kind and helpful by observing the way they read the story of Little Red Riding Hood.

4. FAMILY RELATIONSHIPS

Blood relatives often help each other out. Young Florida scrub jays work with their parents to rear their next brood of offspring, and might receive some territory (and similar support) when they are older. Helping out might reduce the ability of some family members to reproduce, but this can pay off if they receive other benefits in return. This is famously seen among meerkats, who work in a group to look after their young ones.

5. TEAMWORK

Groups of unrelated individuals, like sports teams or army regiments, can work together very well. When one teammate helps another, the whole group benefits. Scientists are still debating whether this kind of cooperation has any influence on the way we and other animals evolve, but Jeff thinks there is evidence that it does.

For Jeff, one of the most wonderful aspects of cooperation is the care that many parents take to nurture, protect, and provide for their offspring. As the emperor penguin and his egg have demonstrated, this behaviour often comes at a very high cost. Any parent knows that there can be an inverse relationship between the number of young and the amount of attention and resources that can be provided. There is also an increase in the amount of care provided, from less to more complex animals.

Most animals without a backbone (including insects) don't look after their young at all, but if they do it's usually the female who guards the young from harm. Fish don't normally do any parenting either, but in some species the female lays her eggs on a male's territory and he stands guard, fanning them in a way that keeps fresh water flowing over them. Male sea horses (which are a kind of fish) even carry their babies around in a pouch.

Tropical amphibians sometimes take care of their young in bizarre ways. It is equally likely to be the father or mother that does the parenting, and they sometimes make great sacrifices in the process. Marsupial frogs keep their eggs in a pouch on their backs, and the Surinam toad actually keeps her babies embedded in her skin. Gastric brooding frogs incubate their eggs in their stomachs, so they can't eat or digest anything for six weeks.

Birds and mammals are by far the most caring parents in the animal kingdom. Baby birds grow very rapidly, so feeding them can be a full-time job, and often both parents are involved in bringing back food. So when hatching time arrives, the male emperor penguin's partner returns to the colony and for the next four months or so they take turns hunting out at sea and feeding regurgitated fish to their chick.

In mammals, the mother pays a very high physical cost of bearing and feeding her young, and usually forms a very strong bond with them. A female elephant, ape, or whale will show strong mourning behaviour if her infant dies or is taken away. Jeff is convinced this display of grief is not just automatic, but shows that the mother understands that an individual she was very attached to is gone.

Being on the outside of a penguin huddle might bring some advantages, but in the fiercest of storms a male penguin might be tempted to spend more time in the pack and skip his turn on the outside. Although playing the game properly will help the group, won't it also reduce his own chances of bringing up a healthy chick? In the face of temptations like this, how did cooperative behaviour become such a powerful force in the living world?

Jeff is fascinated by the checks and balances that keep organisms working together. At every level, from individual cells to whole societies, there are incentives or penalties that keep the relationship going.

There are even mechanisms in our own bodies to stop individual cells from multiplying too rapidly and taking over. If a cell is damaged or loses contact with its neighbours, it dies and is swallowed up by specialist cleaner cells. When these mechanisms break down, benign tumours or even cancer can develop.

When tit-for-tat cooperation is going on, a bit of intelligence is needed to spot cheaters and pick them out later on. If a cleaner wrasse fish gets bored of eating parasites and nibbles on its host instead, it will be chased away. On the other hand, a reliable cleaner may be allowed to visit its host again and again and be rewarded with plenty of food.

Meerkat societies might look cuddly, but they may stay together for reasons that are not quite so cute. An expectant mother harasses the other females, which makes them stressed and less likely to get pregnant. Her pups are now safe from harm by "jealous" females, and there are also lots of babysitters available to help when the pups are a bit older. This is a fairly aggressive way of keeping the group together – a bit more like a truce in the fight for individual survival.

It's harder to explain how a completely unrelated group can work together, but mathematical approaches can help. By modelling the interactions between individuals using computers and mathematical strategies called game theory, researchers can keep track of the different inputs and outcomes. This research has shown that being part of a small, well-connected network can help individuals to thrive, that communication is important, and that reward is better than punishment. It seems that the cooperative penguin isn't making a foolish sacrifice but is actually being very wise.

So what is driving the penguin's behaviour as he squeezes together with his fellow males? We may not know the answer for these particular animals, but we do have some idea about what makes other species look after their young. This research even sheds some light on our own behaviour.

As mammals, we have an inbuilt system that helps us to care. When a mother breastfeeds her child, the hormone oxytocin is released, helping her and her infant to bond. We now know that hormones like this can also affect parents in other species. A female rat normally avoids or even attacks the young of her species, but when she gives birth to her own young, her oxytocin level increases and she behaves in maternal ways, building nests and nursing the pups. A ewe will also steer clear of lambs most of the time, but will start to behave maternally when oxytocin is activated after birth.

For some males, paternal behaviour is helped along by a hormone called vasopressin. After mating, his vasopressin levels increase and he becomes more loyal to his mate and caring towards his offspring. Not all mammals are the same; for example, female mice behave in a maternal way before giving birth, while the males of some species will abandon their mate.

One reason for these differences between animals is that their bodies receive hormones in different ways. The same hormone can cause different behaviours, depending on the effect it has on an individual's brain. The story of the prairie vole and the montane vole is a good example of how this happens.

Prairie voles live in burrows as family groups – or sometimes even extended families. A male guards his mate aggressively and cares for his young, while the female also prefers her mate and acts maternally. Montane voles, on the other hand, are often solitary. They have the same hormones as prairie voles, but the receptors for the hormone signals are in different parts of their brains. In prairie voles the receptors are in regions associated with reward, but in montane voles they are in regions that are important for non-social behaviour. So the same hormone can cause cooperation or not, depending on how animals in that species are wired. There is also evidence that the hormone-detecting mechanisms can vary between individuals in a species, so some individuals are more loyal and caring than others.

One of the most important questions for us is, what does this research on cooperation and hormones mean for our own behaviour and values? Jeff 's students often ask him about this, because it seems to challenge what we think about ourselves and others, the values we hold, and the decisions we make.

There is evidence that oxytocin and vasopressin might have a general role in our own sociability, fostering trust and generosity, but we know virtually nothing about how these hormones affect our sexual or parental behaviour. Jeff responds to his students by sharing the evidence that oxytocin also boosts the immune system and reduces the stress hormone cortisol. We may not know exactly how these hormones affect us, but it seems that we might have an inbuilt mechanism that helps us to flourish when we behave in what most people believe to be an ethically good way.

From a value-based perspective, you could say that doing good creates a fulfilled, joyful, and functionally integrated being. But what about the behaviours that we wouldn't classify as morally good, which can also make people feel good – like excluding others from our group, or acting against other groups? Jeff is quick to point out that our complex brains allow us to override these hormone signals and make more informed choices about what we do and who we want to cooperate with. Our behaviour is influenced by our biochemistry, but not determined by it.

Jeff often quotes C. S. Lewis, who has written that "Love makes vows unasked" and, "Eros is driven to promise what Eros of himself cannot perform." He interprets these statements in a biological sense, saying that although our hormones can make us receptive to being cooperative, we are volatile and frail; we can have a bad day and our oxytocin levels can crash, or our cooperative tendencies can actually lead us to do wrong. Part of being human is that we make active choices whether or not to keep our promises and obey moral rules we think are life-giving, even when our moods might be saying conflicting things.

When a relationship goes beyond our purely biological needs, it is more than cooperation – it is sacrificial giving, or altruism. In all the other examples so far, both individuals gained something, from food and shelter to a general sense of well-being, which makes sense if you are looking at it in evolutionary terms. If every living thing is adapting (by a process of mutation and natural selection) to an environment where resources are limited, then a costly behaviour will only be successful if it improves the survival or welfare of the organism – or its family or group.

What makes us give at times without expecting anything in return? Is there a scientific reason for this sort of behaviour, or does there even have to be one? To start with the science, biologists have been fascinated by altruism and have come up with a few ideas about how it might have developed.

Some researchers wonder if altruism once had its advantages but then the environment changed, and we can only observe the leftover behaviour without seeing the reason why it developed in the first place.

Or maybe most acts that seem altruistic are actually a response to manipulation – like a baby bird clamouring for food from its parent? Most parents will quieten that noise by helping their offspring.

Perhaps altruism has "piggy backed" its way into our behavioural repertoire as part of another trait. For example, does our desire to take care of those close to us simply get out of control so we start trying to take care of everyone?

Was altruism a by-product of some other process? For example, if we developed to take care of our "group", what would happen if that group then expanded through modern communication and the formation of multicultural societies? Potentially, the group could come to include everyone!

Finally, what if natural selection could work on a combination of genes and cultural ideas? For example, if a certain way of being kind was valued among a population, then those who were genetically predisposed to this type of kindness would be more likely to pass on their genes. This would be the teamwork type of cooperation (page 59). And, if cultural input is considered part of the evolutionary process by at least some scientists, then Jeff sees no reason why spiritual ideas can't also be included in the mix.

Jeff has not seen any convincing examples of completely self-giving behaviour outside human societies and has come to the conclusion that it is not just a step up from other forms of cooperation. He believes that our altruistic behaviour is a different phenomenon altogether: a cultural idea that has an impact on the usual evolutionary processes. In other words, we can limit our own survival or the spread of our genes when we help others, but some people choose to do it anyway.

So while the science may be fascinating and helpful to know about, it's not the whole story. One of the differences between us and other animals seems to be that we can choose to do something other than just looking out for ourselves and our own group. We may have predispositions or imbalances that we need to work through, but in the end we are making our own decisions. Jeff believes that what gives us this sense of moral responsibility is our capacity for spirituality.

Science can tell us about some aspects of morality, religious belief or even love, but it cannot tell us what those things are or what we should do about them. The scientific enterprise is fantastically successful at explaining mechanisms but was never intended to answer the question of why we might value certain experiences, or even what it's like for an individual to fully experience certain things. For this reason, Jeff is happy to keep asking questions that can be partly answered by biology, but which also make us think beyond science into other areas of human knowledge and experience.

One final question that Jeff is still curious about is: What happens when we have morally and biologically conflicting impulses? What is it that drives us to make choices that are self-indulgent but don't lead to our personal flourishing, like eating too much or ignoring our families? And what leads us to make good choices? This is another area where biologists have a range of views.

Some scientists believe that our evolutionary development has been driven by forces at both an individual and a group level, and sometimes those forces conflict. Others think that different eras in this development have left us with conflicting behaviours. For example, in a crisis, our lower brain might give us a "fight or flight" response, but other areas of the brain allow us to behave in a more sacrificial way. A third view is that we have constructed social environments that invite us to make poor decisions.

For all of these theories comes the question, where does our will come into this? Why do we sometimes make such poor choices? Is this at all related to the Christian notion of sin? What does it mean to be rescued from the tendency to keep making bad choices, and what is the overall purpose of our lives? We don't know whether biology can help us to understand any of these questions, but they are definitely important ones to investigate.

As we've seen with the case of oxytocin and vasopressin, understanding our biology can help us to understand ourselves a little better and to face up to the very real challenge of making wise decisions. In the end, we have to recognize that we are capable of choosing to do good or do harm – the decision is ours to make.

Jeff's journey through philosophy and biology has left him not just with questions and moral conundrums, but also with an overriding sense of wonder. He firmly believes that all of creation is worthy of our attention, from lichen and frogs to monkeys and people. We need to enjoy that feeling of excitement and curiosity as we explore the living world. The final question these scientists are asking is, then, why do we value the living world at all?

Chapter 8

Living Cities: The value of coral reef ecosystems

As the German army retreated from Paris, Adolf Hitler ordered the destruction of key sites within the city. On a practical level, this was simply a tactic to hold up the advancing Allied armies for a while, depriving them of telephones, bridges, railways, water, and electricity supplies. But as army engineers began to install the bombs, they would have realized that there was a more ideological motive behind their orders. Hitler had intended to destroy priceless cultural treasures, including the palaces, churches, cathedrals, and Eiffel Tower that make Paris so famous.

Anyone who has ever enjoyed exploring a historic city knows that there's something irreplaceable about it. A rich tapestry of architecture has built up over the centuries, with houses piled on top of each other, markets and shops crowded into impossible spaces, parks and gardens hidden behind high walls, coffee houses and eateries on every corner, museums and places of worship, and layer upon layer of memories.

You can rebuild a café, but you cannot replace the umpteen coats of paint that once covered its walls, with layers of grime in between, giving it a "well-loved" appearance that drew in locals as well as tourists. You can remake a wall, but you cannot reconstruct thousands of years of building and repairs, with countless hands shaping the stones, each in their own way.

One version of the events of summer 1944 is that General Dietrich von Choltitz refused to give the order that would set Paris ablaze. This man valued it so much that he preferred to surrender to the

Allies and risk his own life and the lives of his family in the process. Whatever the exact course of events might have been, millions of people are grateful that the planned demolition did not take place.

A city is a wonderful analogy for an ecosystem. Every available space is used, and the cost of acquiring and then maintaining that space is high. The inhabitants work out their relationships in different ways: helping, sharing, or competing for resources. Waste must be disposed of, and fresh resources carried in from outside. Any large city has an impact on the environment and availability of supplies for miles around.

In the same way that a city can be full of priceless treasures, many people think an ecosystem is valuable for its own sake. On a practical level, a forest can provide people with food, water, building materials, and everything else they need in order to survive. But does it also have value for its own sake? The trees themselves may be irreplaceable, and they also provide hiding places for a myriad of other living things. As each organism creates a space for itself, a rich tapestry of life builds up over the centuries – or even millennia – that is beautiful and unique.

Coral reefs are among our most precious ecosystems, covering around 0.2 per cent of the ocean floor, but providing a home for about one-third of all sea-dwelling species. Coral grows so slowly that it can take hundreds or thousands of years to build the huge structures that divers love to explore. Like Paris, the living city is worth investigating at leisure, taking time to look around, discovering surprises and secrets that only the locals know about.

Any reef provides all sorts of spaces where creatures can find shelter and make a living. The coral itself is full of creatures, hidden by their camouflage. Algae grow on every available surface, and are nibbled off by grazing animals. There are animals that work together, like the goby and the shrimp that share a burrow and help each other to hunt. Small fish eat the parasites that live on larger ones, including ocean-going giants that stop off for a quick clean. A large reef can influence the currents and chemistry of a much wider area of ocean.

The marine biologist Dr Margaret W. Miller has spent more than twenty years studying coral and its relationships with other living things. She is fascinated by the variety of organisms involved, the ways they interact with each other, and the different levels of organization – from the water cycle and ocean circulation, right down to microscopic single-celled algae.

Margaret feels immensely privileged to be doing this work, and humbled in the face of such complexity. She often thinks about what ecosystems like these mean and how they should be valued. Should they be cherished for their own sake, and where does that sense of intrinsic value come from? Part of her purpose in studying reefs is to protect them, but, like any conservator of great art, she must first understand what she hopes to preserve.

In living cities, the tower blocks are made of hard coral. Each outcrop is a colony of thousands of tiny individual organisms called polyps, every one inside its own small apartment. Most of the homes are connected by corridors, so the polyps can share nutrients and communicate with each other.

Polyps are small, simple animals with a mouth, gut, and tentacles (see figure 8, page 109). They make their houses by extracting dissolved minerals from the water and converting them into limestone. Every now and then a polyp divides into two and the offspring builds its own limestone home, expanding the colony.

Each species of polyp has its own way of multiplying and relating to its neighbours. Some branch off in all directions, while others are flat like a table. Some grow up in tall columns, and others are like a smooth dome. Some types of polyp are solitary, and soft corals don't need limestone houses at all. This wide range of shapes and sizes is what creates diversity in the reef, providing different spaces for other, non-coral, species to live or hide.

Most corals feed at night by putting out tentacles. Specialized cells on the surface of each tentacle fire out stinging darts to catch any small fish or plankton floating past. When it runs out of space to grow, a coral colony can start a fight with its neighbours. It detects nearby colonies using chemical signals and takes over a new area by ejecting long filaments from its polyps' stomachs, digesting the competitor from the outside in.

Margaret studies elkhorn coral (so-called because of its long, flat branches), which is one of the main reef-builders in the waters around Florida, the Caribbean and the Bahamas. Coral grows so slowly that a very deep reef represents many, many centuries of growth. When hard coral dies, it leaves behind a skeleton that new polyps and other animals can cover with new growth. Over the years, the reef gradually builds up and the living layer can sometimes be more than a kilometre above the sea floor.

Not all of a city's inhabitants are visible to the naked eye. If you ever travel on the Paris Metro you might become home to one of the many viruses or bacteria that circulate in the air conditioning. If you took a splash of water from a fountain, or a scraping from a roof or a crack in a wall, and looked at it under a microscope, you would find plenty of tiny organisms happily existing without anybody being aware of them at all. Some of these microbes are involved in breaking down organic matter, while others are like plants – using solar energy to turn water and carbon dioxide into energy-rich carbohydrates.

Microbes play an extremely important role in the living city. A litre of seawater can contain up to a billion tiny plankton and bacteria. These are the primary energy producers in the ocean, providing food for filter feeders like whales and fish, and recycling nutrients from the dead matter that collects on the sea floor. Some kinds of plankton are like plants, living off the energy they receive from the sun. The rest are tiny animals that drift in the sea their whole lives, or are the young of larger species – including coral.

Coral has a special relationship with a type of plankton: a single-celled algae which is able to take shelter right inside its tissues. Each coral plays host to its own particular species of algae, which gives it its distinctive colour. This works out well for the polyps because the algae recycle the polyps' waste products into useful energy-rich carbohydrates. The algae are also responsible for helping the polyps to make their limestone homes. The relationship of a coral with its plankton is so important that, without them, it will die.

Every centimetre of coral is also covered with tens of millions of bacteria. Each species prefers to live on or in a different part of the polyp, recycling its waste products, crowding out harmful microbes, and providing natural antibiotics. Some of the bacteria make nitrogen-based compounds in the same way that the legumes (clover, beans, and peas) have nitrogen-fixing bacteria in their roots. Sometimes, for reasons that are still mysterious to Margaret and her colleagues, the bacteria turn against their host and cause a fatal disease. The balance between a coral and its microbes is clearly very important for the health of the whole system.

One of the charms of a historic city is the jumble of different types of architecture. An ancient wall is used as the foundation for a new cathedral; a house created in one style is converted to another; and, in times of peace, fortifications may be transformed into spaces for shops and restaurants. Some of these new additions are only possible because parts of the city have been battered by weather or war. Although the wreckage may have been heartbreaking at the time, the gaps that opened up actually created new opportunities for the city to develop.

In a similar way, a living city must be damaged from time to time if it is to stay healthy.

- Most of the white sand on a tropical beach comes from the parrotfish that eat hard coral, grinding its skeleton into tiny chips of limestone and excreting them into the water.

- The bearded fireworm eats hard coral by putting its mouth right over a branch and chewing all the polyps off, leaving only the limestone skeleton behind.

- A little snail called *Coralliophila abbreviata* gathers in groups, pumping enzymes onto the coral to digest it.

- Damselfish sometimes create algae gardens, nipping off polyps here and there when they encroach on their special patch of seaweed.

These regular mild attacks are what make a reef varied and colourful, and even the occasional devastation can be healthy. The pounding waves caused by a hurricane break open new spaces; El Niño warming events kill large areas of coral; and predator species can have rare population surges and eat more coral than usual. As the reef recovers, species that might have been squeezed out can find some room to grow. Learning more about the delicate balance between predator and prey can help marine biologists to understand why new disturbances often devastate whole reefs.

A city like Paris needs people to inhabit and enjoy its spaces. There must be people who can look around, eat out, and shop. People should want to make and build beautiful things. Without the right combination of economics, weather, politics, and so on, the whole place would fold.

Each coral species also has a set of conditions it needs to thrive. Elkhorn coral is fast-growing, and in the right circumstances it can grow up to ten centimetres a year. What it needs is:

- a hard surface to grow on above the sea floor, away from sand and sediment;

- clear, clean, well-circulated water;

- shallow water, so sunlight can reach the algae inside the polyps;

- a temperature of 19 to 30°C (66°F to 86°F), so the algae can survive;

- the right balance of chemicals in the water, so the polyps can extract minerals from it.

Growth is not the only way for a reef to expand. When a branch is broken off in a storm, it can start growing again by itself – but only if it falls in a suitable place. The new colony is genetically identical to its parent, so to stay diverse and healthy a coral also has to reproduce sexually.

Once or twice a year, elkhorn coral makes sperm and eggs (both from the same polyp) and releases them into the sea. There are mechanisms in place to stop self-fertilization, so breeding can only be successful if two unrelated colonies are near enough to each other – as well as spawning at the same time. If coral babies happen to be made, they will drift through the sea for a few days as plankton. Any that manage to survive long enough and settle in a good place will eventually grow into a polyp, and perhaps a whole new colony (see figure 9, page 110). Coral breeding is a fragile process, but it obviously works, because reefs have flourished all over the globe – from north to south as well as in tropical regions.

Sadly, many cities around the world have been reduced to rubble at some point in their history. If the circumstances are right, some rebuilding might happen spontaneously as new homes, businesses, and social spaces spring up among the wreckage. More often, a government or city council might need to provide advice, funding, and leadership for large projects. Unless people are involved who truly understand how cities operate, the restoration may not return it to even part of its former glory.

Margaret's role is similar to a post-war city planner. She wants to become so at home with reef ecosystems that she can help repair them. Leaving things alone is often the best strategy in conservation, but sometimes the damage is too great to heal itself – especially with slow-growing organisms like coral.

One of the simplest ways of helping a reef to regrow is by "coral gardening". This can be as easy as using cable ties or resin to stick a fragment of coral back on the reef. Clumps of coral can even be propagated, like cuttings, making thousands of colonies in a sustainable way. When nurseries are set up in safe environments, large numbers of fragments can be monitored and kept free of predators and algae until they are strong enough to be transplanted. Like replanting a forest, all of these interventions will take many years to have any effect, but so far the results are promising.

Another way to help the reef recover is by protecting fish and sea urchins that eat the seaweed that spreads rapidly over damaged coral. In the 1980s, a deadly disease almost wiped out black long-spined urchins in the Caribbean. The reefs became carpeted with algae, especially in areas where overfishing was already having an impact. Thankfully, over three decades later, the population has begun to recover, the seaweed is being eaten away, and coral is starting to regrow.

As well as being town planners, Margaret and her team act as midwives. One of the problems with elkhorn coral at the moment is that sexual reproduction is failing. As a result, the colonies in each area are becoming more identical at a genetic level. When the population becomes too small and inbred, it is even more difficult for eggs and sperm from different parents to meet.

We know from agriculture that if everyone uses the same variety of a crop in one area, a single disease can destroy the entire harvest. In the same way, coral must keep outbreeding or it could be wiped out very quickly. So midwifery has become the newest form of reef restoration, but it involves far more challenging techniques than taking cuttings.

Every summer, Margaret goes diving at night, when the coral is spawning, collects sperm and eggs from several different areas, mixes them together, and brings them back to her lab. The fertilized eggs are held in very clean water for a few days, until they develop into larvae and start swimming around. Although they are still less than a millimetre wide and completely transparent, this exploring behaviour is a sign that the larvae are ready to be released.

The marine midwives have tried several different ways of reintroducing coral babies into the sea. One way is to put them in a net around a dead elkhorn branch, so there are plenty of suitable places to grow. After a week or two the larvae will settle on the reef as polyps, and be colonized by the algae that give them their colour. Another method is to present them with a small piece of concrete to land on, then attach that to the reef. The survival rate is not more than a tiny percentage so far, but even that is a significant step toward conserving these valuable animals.

Some city centres are so unique that they have been given protected status. At UNESCO World Heritage Sites, special efforts are made to preserve the heritage that has built up over the centuries and restore it if it becomes damaged. A similar process can happen for living cities, but using very different methods.

Dr Bob Sluka, a friend and colleague of Margaret's, heads up the International Marine and Coastal Conservation programme for the Christian conservation organization A Rocha. For many years he has worked in marine reserves: protected areas set up to safeguard rich and vulnerable ecosystems – acting as a living reservoir for the surrounding area. Bob has seen first-hand that protection from overfishing and other damage can help reefs recover their natural balance and fruitfulness. The fact that the fish and their young can move in and out freely also means that the reserves replenish fish stocks for miles around.

One of A Rocha's marine projects is based in Kenya, at the Mwamba Field Study Centre in the Watamu Marine National Park. The protected site covers reefs, lagoons, mangrove forests, and sea grass beds. Although the area is still recovering from damage, visitors today can see a huge variety of fish and coral species, moray eels, three species of turtle, manta rays, octopus, reef sharks, and whale sharks.

Bob is supporting in-depth scientific research in Watamu, so that he and his colleagues can get to know the reef systems and find ways of managing them more effectively. They have already found that the rock pools on the beach act as nurseries for the fish that will eventually live out on the reef.

Bob and his team have also kick-started beach clean-ups and advocacy projects with the local community. Building, tree felling, and agriculture all affect the water quality in the bay, so land-based initiatives are important. The effects of climate change will be much harder to deal with, but marine parks are a good start in learning how to live more sustainably on the ocean.

For Margaret, life as a marine biologist has given her a deep sense of humility. Understanding just a few aspects of living cities is a huge challenge, let alone attempting to restore them. She is well aware of the scale of the problem she is attempting to tackle. "It is a daunting task to try to help restore these complex systems. We have so much more to learn, but everything I do understand helps me to appreciate them even more."

Scientific research can also help us to recognize the true value of coral reefs. Such rich ecosystems provide us with a whole range of benefits, from protecting shorelines to providing homes for edible species and offering an experience of great beauty. But many scientists also believe these places are worth treasuring for their own sake.

This sense of intrinsic value resonates with Margaret's own faith, and especially the idea that God has a loving relationship with all of creation. Right at the beginning of the Bible, God gives humankind a mandate to care for the natural world. We have a unique role in looking after living things, perhaps because we have the ability to be so destructive when we forget that responsibility.

The other challenge in Margaret's work is keeping a sense of hope in the face of overwhelming losses to the coral population and the scale of some of the threats. Reefs may be worth protecting, but is that even possible? Margaret finds hope in her belief that God is in ultimate control of what is happening, and that he has a purpose for earth and its inhabitants. Natural systems can recover their fruitfulness, and they are being preserved or restored in many places around the world. This flourishing is a sign of even greater things to come.

Every scientist featured here has expressed some theological or biblical reflections about their work and the questions of meaning or purpose that their research raises for them. Before we go on to explore these ideas and look at what the ultimate purpose of the living world might be, it's worth hearing from a theologian. Alister McGrath is one of the foremost voices in the science and religion dialogue. The fact that he started his working life as a scientist means that he is well equipped for a conversation about purpose, meaning, and biology.

Chapter 9

Surprised by Meaning:
Can the world say anything
about God?[10]

The most famous photo of earth from space, "The Blue Marble", was taken by the crew of the Apollo 17 in 1972. We are so used to seeing pictures like this today that it is easy to forget quite how new this perspective of our planet is. It was only in the 1940s that the first pictures were snapped from unmanned rockets in near-earth orbit and stitched together to show a patch of cloud here, a piece of a continent there, and the surface of the earth curving away into the distance. These grainy, low-resolution black-and-white images gave people the first glimpse of the place we live in from a completely new angle.

The story that science now tells us about the universe is truly awe-inspiring. It begins with the Big Bang and the formation of stars, which produced different kinds of atoms. Atoms combined to form molecules, and those molecules came together in increasing levels of complexity, eventually forming replicating cells. Cells joined together to form ever-more diverse kinds of organisms, which interact in multi-layered ecosystems. Curiosity provokes us to explore the worlds that are uncovered by science, and wonder is both a result and a driver of that exploration.

So far we have encountered six scientists who are fascinated by what they see in the living world. Their discoveries make them ask scientific questions about the order and complexity they find, but it

---

10　This is the title of one of Alister McGrath's books, in which he writes about how both science and faith can help us make sense of life.

also prompts more philosophical or theological questions. What is life for, and what does it mean?

The previous chapters will have raised different questions for different people. Are you curious about the details of the research, or the gaps in our scientific understanding that might be filled in the future? Did the panorama of life, from the first glimmerings of life on a rocky planet to whole ecosystems, give you a sense of awe that makes you value life on earth even more than ever? Or does the emergence of cooperative societies make you ask, "What for?"

Before delving into each scientist's own views on questions like this, it's worth looking at the story of a scientist who made a career change to theology. Alister McGrath has had the opportunity to think very deeply about the questions raised by science, and it's interesting to see where his investigations have taken him.

Gazing at earth from space often gives an astronaut the "overview effect": a feeling of awe, a realization of the unity of everything on the planet, and a sense of its fragility. For some, this experience of literally seeing the bigger picture leads them to change their beliefs and practices when they return to solid ground. This is just one example of how being exposed to a wider perspective can affect a person's outlook on life.

As a child, Alister was gripped by a sense of wonder at the living world. He was curious about astronomy, so he made himself a small telescope and used it to observe the moons of Jupiter. When someone gave him an old microscope, he started looking at the details of plants and tiny organisms in pond water. Falling in love with the beauty and fascination of the world around him, he decided his future was in the lab.

At first, Alister thought a good scientist should embrace atheism, but that was before he began to explore the philosophy of science. He later wrote, "I had stepped through a door, and could not escape the new world I now inhabited."[11] Scientists find the mechanisms of how things work, but the tools of science cannot answer questions about meaning or purpose. Looking at his own experience of the world, Alister found that atheism was one way of interpreting the data,

---

11   Derek R. Nelson, Joshua M. Moritz, and Ted Peters (eds), *Theologians in Their Own Words* (Minneapolis: Fortress Press, 2013).

but not the only way – or even the one he found most convincing. Having embraced the view that life is a cosmic accident, it was a huge surprise for him to encounter evidence for a God of meaning and purpose.

As a student at Oxford University, Alister faced questions about the relationship between science and faith. Charles Coulson, the professor of theoretical chemistry, reassured him that faith is not about trying to find God in the gaps of our scientific knowledge, but that God makes sense of the whole picture. In fact, if God really is the creator of the whole universe, then science should help us to learn more about him. If scientists and theologians are both searching for the truth, then the two should be compatible. These are the sorts of ideas that drove Alister to study theology.

We all look at the world in a certain way, whether we are aware of it or not. That's one reason why astronauts experience the overview effect in such a powerful way. We compare everything we see or learn to what we already know, so when we are exposed to something radically new it can completely reshape the boundaries of our thinking.

Alister made the switch to theology by working on a degree in this subject at the same time as a PhD in biophysics. As he looked at the world through the lens of theology, science became simply a useful tool for understanding how things work. He realized that scientists limit themselves to aspects of the world that can be observed or measured, and described using mathematical equations or theoretical models. So people of all faiths and none can work on scientific projects together, because their faith will affect their behaviour but not the outcomes of their experiments.

Alister began his academic career by studying historical theology, but soon moved on to start working out the relationship between science and faith. He knew from experience that both scientists and theologians believe there is a reality out there, waiting to be discovered. That reality is completely independent of us and is not affected by anything we think or do.

Within science, each investigation has a different starting point. An astronomer begins with atoms and physical forces, while a biologist might start at the level of molecules and cells. We have to make assumptions about the world and put limits on what is being examined, otherwise we would be too overwhelmed to begin anything. But if we operated from the same point of view all the time, we might lose sight of the big picture.

Each method of study has its own toolbox of techniques. Philosophers use arguments, historians look for primary sources, literary theorists assess texts – and, like science, there will be different ways of functioning within these disciplines. For Alister, one way of picturing these ways of thinking is to see them as levels in the same reality. Each method examines one of these levels and ignores the rest. In the same way that a print can be made by adding multiple layers of paint on top of each other, it takes a complete set of levels to show us the full meaning of reality.

A reality scientists get to experience is the beauty of the systems they study. Some of the things they enjoy might also be attractive to a non-scientist, like the minute organisms in pond water, or they might be more specialized, like an elegant mathematical equation. In the last few years, Alister has spent a lot of time thinking about whether the beauty of creation can tell us something about the beauty of a creator. Or, more generally, if we believe there is a God, can we learn anything about him from the things he has made?

For Alister, the best approach to this question is to look at the living world from the point of view of faith in God – perhaps as a thought experiment if you don't believe in God personally. This saves us pretending that we can look at things from a neutral viewpoint, when in reality everyone has a point of view that informs the way they think. So we could ask: Do Christian ideas about creation make sense of what biochemists, ecologists, or developmental biologists know about the world? Or: If God exists, then does that make sense of what psychologists have discovered about children having a natural belief in a deity? Do the things that are revealed by the tools of science become clear in the light of theology?

In the Old Testament, God is described as bringing order out of chaos. At the beginning of Genesis the world is described as "formless and empty"; then the narrative tells of God adding layer upon layer of structure and pattern. The Bible is a pre-scientific text, so it's no surprise that we don't find any kind of scientific detail in there. But, having looked at the biblical account of creation with its patterns of forming and filling, we might expect to find some kind of order in the world – and that is exactly what we do see.

It also makes sense that the God who gives his subjects freedom might choose to use random processes (like the ones Rhoda Hawkins studies in Chapter 4) to allow things to "design themselves". And if the processes of natural selection are heading in the direction of increasing complexity, and toward certain solutions or functions, this resonates with the idea of God having a purpose for the living world.

This type of thought experiment works for Alister. Biology alone is not enough to make him believe in God. But the processes of the living world are compatible with belief in a loving creator who has not just made life but has also given it a meaning and a purpose of its own.

Alister is convinced that we should use the language of purpose in science. Biologists often use purposeful-sounding words when they describe the organisms they study. They might say that a certain group of proteins all serve the same purpose inside the cell, evolutionary processes happen for certain reasons, or every creature acts in its own interests.

Some scientists have argued that this language can only be used in a metaphorical way. They say it might look as if animals, cells, or proteins have a purpose, but they really don't. Others disagree because many biological processes do actually seem to be fulfilling a purpose. For example, they would say that the leopard got its spots because they helped its ancestors to hunt; each of the organs in our bodies contributes to our overall health; and an amoeba eats bacteria because it needs energy to survive.

Even if biological processes have a functional or scientifically described "purpose", some people still insist that we avoid using that word because it's so strongly associated in most people's minds with deeper ideas about meaning and value. In other words, science is about mechanisms, so we shouldn't get it mixed up with ideas about philosophy or religion. Not everyone agrees.

The work of Stephen Freeland, Rhoda Hawkins, and Simon Conway Morris seems to show that the emergence of life in the universe was somehow inevitable. Cell biologists like Jeff Hardin are well aware of the directional processes that shape embryos, and of the fact that each cell has a specific and essential function in the dance of development. Jeff Schloss and Margaret Miller know how organisms can work together in complex relationships to reach a common goal of survival and reproduction.

None of these processes tells us anything about its ultimate meaning or purpose in a philosophical or theological way, but they all seem to be heading in a certain direction. Perhaps there are two kinds of purpose here. Biological purpose is about processes that are for something: striving to reach the goal of flourishing in a certain way, whether that is a cheetah eating gazelles or a bacterium slithering to a particular point in a petri dish where there is food. Ultimate purpose, on the other hand, is something that scientific data may hint at, but cannot speak to – for that we need to look to other levels of reality.

One of Alister's student holidays took him to Iran. There was a trip one night across a vast desert, avoiding the heat of the day by attempting to sleep in a rickety bus. Perhaps inevitably, the bus broke down. People got out while the engine was being fixed and began to wander about, looking for ways to kill time. Alister's eyes turned upward, and whatever feelings he had been experiencing before – frustration, tiredness, fear, or boredom – quickly turned to awe when he saw the stars as he had never seen them before.

I recently met a student from that area whose face, when we asked her about the night sky in the desert, expressed everything Alister must have felt when he saw it for himself. It is beautiful, awe inspiring, overwhelming, wonderful, and perhaps a little terrifying. No one could ever forget that sky.

For some people, a sense of wonder is an end in itself. But for Alister, it leads him to ask theological questions. Stepping back and taking in as much as possible of the rich and multi-layered reality of the world, it is possible to see how scientific knowledge fits into the bigger picture. What is the ultimate purpose of the living world?

Much of Alister's work is about exploring the places where science informs faith, and vice versa. Most of all, it is about presenting a view of reality that makes sense of everything we know and experience. Scientists don't tend to write about these sorts of things in their papers, but they are worth sharing. In the final chapter, the people whose discoveries we have shared will give their own perspectives on science, faith, and the ultimate purpose of the universe.

Chapter 10

Biology and Belief: A journey through science and faith

Well before our current travelling boom, and before even the first road maps of Britain were made, a man called John Ray went on an expedition around the country, collecting plants. The year was 1658, when reliable toll roads had not yet been introduced, carriages were uncomfortable, and there was always a danger of robbers or highwaymen. Despite the potential setbacks, over the next decade Ray made himself one of the best-travelled scientists (or natural philosophers, as they were called at that time) in the country, going as far as Italy in his search for new samples.

Ray was a lecturer at Trinity College Cambridge, and took up botany when he became ill and had to take long walks or go out riding for his health. Having started out teaching mathematics, Greek, and humanities, he became famous for his work on plants. He wrote the first modern textbook on the subject and coined the terms "petal" and "pollen".

Lecturers in seventeenth-century Cambridge had to become priests in the Church of England, but Ray's ordination was no box-ticking exercise. He saw science as a way to serve God, and even delivered a series of talks on the *Wisdom of God in the Works of Creation* in Trinity College chapel. Not all of Ray's ideas about the relationship between science and faith have stood the test of time, but his science was excellent and his faith was sincere. In the introduction to one of his books on plants, Ray wrote:

> We would urge men of University standing to spare a brief
> interval from other pursuits for the study of nature... so
> that they can gain wisdom in it at first hand... there is for
> a free man no occupation more worthy and delightful than
> to contemplate the beauteous works of nature and honour
> the infinite wisdom and goodness of God.

A century after Ray, science was finally established as a profession in its own right. Theological language is no longer used in scientific publications, and people of all religions and none can get involved. It's worth celebrating the fact that careers in science are now open to a wider population, but there should still be a place for hearing the human stories – including those about faith – behind the discoveries.

All the scientists whose work is covered here are Christians. We have already had some hints about their questions and thoughts on meaning and purpose, but does their work interact with faith on a more personal level, as it did for John Ray? And where do they go for answers to their questions? It's time to hear about these people's own journeys through science and faith.

Dr Ruth M. Bancewicz (Chapter 2. Inner Worlds)

Born: Glasgow, UK
Studied at: Aberdeen and Edinburgh Universities
Current position: Church Engagement Director, The Faraday Institute for Science and Religion, Cambridge
Previous roles: Postdoctoral Research Fellow, Wellcome Trust Centre for Cell Biology, University of Edinburgh; Development Officer, Christians in Science
Special interests: Beauty, wonder, the positive relationship between science and faith
Also likes: Being outdoors, running, playing the violin

Like John Ray, I became interested in the living world and how it works just by being exposed to it. I grew up climbing all the hills we could find near our home in South Manchester, being taught the names of plants and trees by my mum, and foraging for anything we knew was edible. At school I found that I was good at science and loved the idea that I could study biology full-time.

I was also keen to find out whether or not God is real. I kept my eyes open and found plenty of support for faith in the answers I saw to prayer, positive changes in the way people I knew lived, and especially the way my own family operated. I had been taught to be sure of my facts before I committed to anything, and this heap of evidence made me happy to accept the truth of Christianity.

At university, my eyes were opened to the incredible level of detail inside the cell. I fell in love with the creativity of molecular biology – the study of DNA and proteins – and the way that simple biochemical techniques could be used to reveal the secrets of these inner worlds. The more I learned, the more I began to ask questions about how science and faith interacted.

Unlike Ray, I had not yet learned to worship God with science, but that began to change when a professor at my church introduced me to an organization called Christians in Science. I was hugely encouraged to see the list of past presidents, each of whom had a career in science behind them. These people had already tackled the main questions about science and faith and were willing to share their thoughts publicly.

As I went on to explore the world of the zebrafish and how its eyes developed, I kept searching for answers about science and faith. I was looking for people to talk to, but I didn't do very well at finding them. I was finally motivated by a job advert, and when I started working for Christians in Science, I was able to ask all the questions I liked. I realized that not only can science and faith work together, but they also help each other in their own way.

One of my main motivations for writing this book was to help others become more involved in the discussion. By giving a group of successful scientists the opportunity to communicate their own thinking about faith, I hope to inspire some more fruitful conversations than the ones I have had in the past. Each one of these people has their own unique perspective to bring to the table, but there are also some commonalities between what they say.

Science and faith

On any journey there are features that make a regular appearance. There might be a familiar tree species or type of building that pops up in the scenery every now and then. Other things might stay with you the entire time, like the structure of the road, types of cars, or road signs. For John Ray, some of the similarities on his travels would have come from the same plants sprouting in different places.

For us, there have been commonalities in the ways people think about their work and faith. The scientists here all share a common sense of wonder and awe at the world. They experience these feelings at different times and respond to them in different ways. For Jeff Hardin there is often wonder at visual beauty: "When I see an amazing image that our lab or some other lab has generated... those cause me to stop, to pause with wonder, to stand really rapt in awe..." For Rhoda Hawkins, on the other hand, wonder is that sense of enquiry that drives her work forward and makes her get up in the morning when things aren't going well. Both kinds of wonder are important, and everyone experiences them at different points in their career.

Of course, all the scientists here think science and faith are compatible, and can help each other. Some of them have explained this relationship in terms of meaning and mechanism. Science is all about understanding the mechanisms for things: why does the plant grow, or the cloud form in the sky? But science cannot say what these things mean to us, beyond the purely functional. We need plants for food, but a particular plant could take on a special meaning for a person because it is associated with memories of good times in the past.

Another commonality between the scientists is their appreciation of order, and this is, of course, part of good science. The world is ordered, and we try to find ways to explain where those patterns come from – on a number of different levels, both to do with mechanism and meaning.

The sense of purpose and meaning we find in life – and especially to explain why life arose in the first place – is a very personal thing, but every scientist here has that sense of purpose and can explain why they believe in it. Each of these unique perspectives can help us to plot a route through the relationship between science and faith.

The path meanders a little as it passes through the realms of personal history and experience, but together the different perspectives described here can help us make sense of science and faith.

Professor Stephen Freeland
(Chapter 3. One in a Million?)

Born: Nairobi, Kenya
Studied at: Oxford, York, and Cambridge Universities
Current position: Director of Individualized Study, University of Maryland Baltimore County (UMBC)
Previous roles: Postdoctoral Fellow, Princeton University; Professor of Bioinformatics, UMBC; Project Manager, NASA Astrobiology Institute, University of Hawaii
Special interests: The origins of the genetic code, the interface of science and religion, and using the creative arts to visualize and communicate social science, natural science, and engineering.
Also likes: Gardening, DIY

With a father who taught biology before retraining as a Methodist minister, science and Christianity have always been part of Stephen Freeland's life. Both scientists and theologians are interested in probing deeper into the mysteries of life, each in their own particular ways. One point of contact between science and faith is the belief – which Stephen embraces – that God created by establishing physical laws. Seeing order in the world, Stephen thinks it is clear that the forces inside an atom, the strength of gravity, and all the other regularities in the way matter and energy behave, were an essential ingredient in the origin of life.

All living things on our planet share the same system of DNA and protein, and it appears to be very special: optimized for the purpose of passing on information from one generation to another. Because the materials and physical forces that shaped the genetic code are the same all over the universe, he thinks that, if life arose on another planet, it might contain a similar sort of code.

For Stephen, the God of the Bible is one of wonder and surprise, sometimes unexpected, and often beyond our understanding. He is astonished by what he finds in his work on astrobiology, and the inspiration for his research comes from "a loving creator God whose universe I am exploring". He often goes back to these words from the Bible – "In the beginning was the Word, and the Word was with God, and the Word was God" – explaining that, "Although we translate Logos as 'Word', it has such rich meaning in the Greek from which it comes, including logic and the general approach to finding meaning about any topic that gives us the 'logy' of Biology or Geology."

Stephen believes that science is part of our God-given capacity for understanding the order and patterns in the universe God created. Like Alister McGrath, Stephen is not interested in scientific arguments for God, but in the ways in which science points to questions about God. These questions can prompt us to look to other areas of life for answers, and, for many, these questions lead back to God.

"There is a lot of truth," Stephen says, "in the statement that faith is about meaning, and science tells us about how things happened, their mechanisms and histories." For him, "meaning and purpose require us to step beyond science, into whatever realm you choose to put your faith in… Faith is a deeper truth… and I am convinced that I can see God transform lives in ways I haven't seen for politics or philosophies, so that confirms it works for me."

Dr Rhoda Hawkins
(Chapter 4. Artistic Molecules)

Born: London, UK
Studied at: Oxford and Leeds Universities
Current positions: Senior Lecturer in Physics, University of Sheffield; Visiting Lecturer, The African Institute for Mathematical Sciences (AIMS)
Previous roles: Postdoctoral Researcher, University of Bristol, UK; Postdoctoral Researcher, Université Pierre et Marie Curie/Institut Curie, France; Postdoctoral Researcher, Institute for Atomic and Molecular Physics (AMOLF), The Netherlands
Special interests: Biological physics, active matter, soft matter, science and religion, wonder
Also likes: Running, hills, impressionist paintings

The process of asking questions has been a driving force in Rhoda Hawkins' life. In her work, she loves challenging herself and pushing her science to the limits. In her faith, she also tries to interrogate what she believes. "How does prayer work? Why does God only seem to answer some of my prayers? How does God interact with us?" There have been periods of doubting and exploring different answers, reading, and talking to people about their own views. Those times have always strengthened her faith in the long run.

She loves these words from the Bible:

> Do you not know? Have you not heard? The LORD is the everlasting God, the Creator of the ends of the earth. He will not grow tired or weary, and his understanding no one can fathom.
> **Isaiah 40:28**

She says, "As well as speaking of God as the Creator, it has the suggestion of questioning in it, and the point that God is beyond our understanding. There's also the comparison that, unlike us when we work hard, God does not get tired or weary."

When Rhoda manages to describe one of the cell's intricate mechanisms with a mathematical equation, she feels that she is seeing the mind of God. For her, the beauty and complexity of the world, and the simplicity of its underlying physical laws and principles, are amazing. "This leads me to worship the creator who made these amazing things and processes in the universe."

Rhoda was drawn into science by her sense of wonder at the world, and her belief that it was made by someone good. What better way to find out more about God than to study what he has made? If faith helped Rhoda's interest in science to grow, that influence also goes the other way. "I don't think there's any scientific proof for the existence of God… But if we believe that God made the world, then we can find out more about what he's like from what we see in nature."

On a very small scale, Rhoda can see the random or unpredictable movement of molecules, which has led some people to say that life is equally random. On a larger scale, though, things can be ordered and purposeful, achieving certain functions. Rhoda is quite happy to use the word "purpose" in a more theological sense: "It is possible for God to use random processes to make the world and yet still have purpose in that."

Rhoda believes that our understanding of the world will always be partial. Progress in both scientific research and theology gradually draws us closer to reality, but we will never completely understand it because our finite minds cannot fully grasp the power and scale of either the world around us or its creator.

Professor Jeff Hardin
(Chapter 5. Dance of the Cells)

Born: Milwaukee, USA
Studied at: Michigan State University, International School of Theology, and University of California Berkeley
Current position: Raymond E. Keller Professor of Zoology and Chair of Integrative Biology, University of Wisconsin-Madison
Previous role: Postdoctoral Fellow, Department of Zoology, Duke University
Special interests: Cell and developmental biology, theology, science and religion, beauty
Also likes: Playing classical clarinet, singing, tennis, hiking

---

Jeff Hardin is somewhat unusual as a scientist because, in between degrees in science, he spent some time studying theology. His time away from the lab provided a solid intellectual foundation for his faith and helped him to think about the deep connections between Christianity and science. As a seminary student, he also studied philosophy, which shows him how science fits into a wider context.

For Jeff, seeing beauty in the living world is a pointer to God himself, the author of everything that is beautiful and true. To him, the microscope images of the worm embryos he studies are as beautiful as a painting by an old master or stained glass in a cathedral. "When I see an amazing image from the lab, it causes me to stop, pause with wonder and stand rapt in awe, and thank God who lies behind all of this beauty."

To take just one example, Jeff's work in understanding how embryos develop feeds into his thinking about one of the most unique and important aspects of Christian theology – the incarnation. "For this to be true, Jesus of Nazareth is human, and so he went through the very same steps of development that all of us went through, and that fills me with a sense of complete amazement, and helps me to see just how thoroughly and completely God identifies with us as human beings."

Our small and fragile beginnings can lead to a sense of humility, but that is balanced by the knowledge that God's plans include each one of us. Jeff recognizes that the universe is greater than he is, but it is also deeply meaningful. Like all the scientists involved in this book, he believes that God used evolutionary processes to accomplish the task of creation over a period of billions of years. "Knowing that I am a part of something absolutely huge... is a cause of excitement, and enhances my own sense of worship as a Christian."

As Stephen Freeland said, you have to step beyond science to think about meaning and purpose, so although most people don't have time for a second degree, many of the people involved in the conversation about science and faith have found themselves reading outside their own subject.

Professor Simon Conway Morris
(Chapter 6. Map of Life)

Born: London, UK
Studied: Bristol and Cambridge Universities
Current position: Emeritus Professor of Palaeobiology, University of Cambridge
Previous roles: Professor of Evolutionary Palaeobiology, Cambridge University; Research Fellow, St John's College, Cambridge; Lecturer in Earth Sciences, Open University
Special interests: The first fossil animals, constraints on evolution, emergence of complexity
Also likes: G. K. Chesterton, a glass of wine

Simon Conway Morris' route into faith as a student involved reading the theological and philosophical works of C. S. Lewis, Dorothy Sayers, J. R. R. Tolkien, and G. K. Chesterton. When he learned about the historical reliability of the biblical accounts of Jesus' life, death, and resurrection, these narratives rang true. Having searched deeply, asking difficult questions and exploring realities beyond science, he found a way of making sense of the world that works best for him, and has identified as a Christian ever since.

Simon's work in palaeontology – exploring the connections and similarities between organisms – has highlighted for him the difference between scientific and other kinds of evidence. In a sense, science allows us to investigate the world, while faith asks, "Why is the world organized like this?"

Some people think there is no meaning in the universe, but Simon is convinced there is, and that there is even a faint possibility of seeing purpose in the process. He is constantly surprised by the evidence in his own work that "we as humans have a very strong sense of purpose, and yet seem to have come out of a universe apparently without purpose". But there are hints that evolution has deeper organizational principles behind it, and may actually be quite an ordered process. What if this process was always going to produce intelligent beings in the end: beings who were capable of encountering God? Is there a resonance between science and faith here that makes sense?

When it comes to finding out about God from his creation, Simon agrees with Alister McGrath that the best approach is to see which worldview makes the most sense of everything we know about the world, including science. For example, the natural world is ordered in a way that has allowed creative and conscious beings to emerge who understand rationality, logic, and mathematics. All of this is consistent with the existence of the God described in the Bible.

Like Rhoda, Simon often wrestles with difficult questions. For him, these uncertainties are not a weakness; they simply reflect who God is – that he is intimately near but in some way unknowable. Faith is a process of learning: an adventure of exploration that has scarcely begun. "Every time you think you've got something sorted out, somebody will remind you there is another perspective on things."

Professor Jeff Schloss
(Chapter 7. The Snuggle for Existence)

Studied: Wheaton College and Washington University
Current positions: Distinguished Professor of Biology; T. B. Walker

Chair of Natural and Behavioral Sciences, and Director of the Center for Faith, Ethics and Life Sciences, Westmont College; BioLogos Senior Scholar

Previous roles: Crosson Fellow, University of Notre Dame Center for Philosophy of Religion; Plumer Fellow, St Anne's College Oxford; Senior Fellow, Emory University Center for Law and Religion

Special interests: Evolution of unselfish behaviour and moral systems, theological implications of Darwinism, adaptations of organisms to dehydration

Also likes: Surfing

Jeff Schloss's search for answers led him to study philosophy. As a child, he was fascinated by science. He loved all the experiment kits his family bought for him, but when it came to choosing a career, he was asking too many questions about meaning and purpose that science couldn't answer.

During a break in his studies, Jeff encountered Christianity through the kindness of a stranger. After wrestling with the arguments for and against faith, he was finally convinced. Today, he believes that "Not only is there a God who orders creation and gives it and our lives purpose, but God reaches out to us with the invitation for intimacy and acceptance by him."

As a new Christian, Jeff began to find that some of his questions about meaning and purpose were being answered. He realized that he could enjoy science again for the sheer fun of it. He started studying biology and found that science is complementary to belief in the God who made everything. Faith can give an added impetus for studying the natural world, while the natural world itself is a reflection of the wisdom and goodness of its creator. This way of delighting in science became a new driving force for Jeff's academic career.

As he delved deeper into biology, Jeff found that science was raising new philosophical questions for him. He began to explore the area of cooperation: not just the kindness of strangers but also ways of seeing kindness in other animals, and even plants and bacteria. What might prompt them to work together in these ways, or even to give without receiving anything in return? His work since then has become a blend of both biology and philosophy, as he attempts to unravel these issues.

Jeff has become interested in what happens when we allow faith to prompt questions that can be answered by science. For example, "Is there such a thing as natural beneficence? Is the world essentially characterized by what we would call 'natural-' or 'non-moral evil', or is it in fact constructed so that something more positive emerges out of the natural world?"

As a child, Jeff heard his family discussing what life was about, and what was involved in living "the good life". He now believes that genuine self-giving behaviour is possible, that it is a choice, and that it comes with rewards for both physical and spiritual well-being.

Dr Margaret Miller (Chapter 8. Living Cities)

Born: Seattle, USA
Studied: Indiana University and University of North Carolina, Chapel Hill
Current position: Research Director of the coral conservation group SECORE International
Previous roles: Postdoctoral Researcher, University of Miami; Ecologist, Protected Resources Division/Benthic Ecosystem Assessment and Research at the National Oceanic and Atmospheric Administration's Southeast Fisheries Science Center, Miami, Florida
Special interests: Coral reef ecology, conservation, scuba diving
Also likes: Hiking, cooking, travelling, canoeing

Margaret Miller has always found science helpful to her faith, and vice versa, but at an outward level they have often been very separate activities. As she has gained confidence in both areas, Margaret has had opportunities to speak about faith in the scientific arena, and to bring her scientific knowledge into the church context. "I had always conceptualized them as complementary, but to be in a position to discuss that has been very enriching."

As a marine ecologist working on coral reef conservation, Margaret is struck by the parallel ways in which science and theology describe what's happening in the world. The words people use are different, and they come from different ways of thinking about the world, but they have somewhat similar meanings and can lead to roughly parallel courses of action.

In theology there is "fruitfulness" in the world, but there is also "sin", and the living world must be "tended and cared for". In scientific language the world is "resilient", but there is "ecosystem degradation", and it must be "conserved and restored". It's interesting to hear these two conversations playing out, and, of course, people like Margaret have an important role to play in both of them.

For example, one of the reasons Margaret feels so drawn to study the living world is that she sees God reflected in his creation. Among the beautiful reefs, she sees God's beauty. For her, the different creatures interacting together are a way of seeing provision by God for every living thing.

Speaking about purpose, Margaret is immediately concerned with the big picture of life on earth, and where coral reefs might fit into that. "When ecosystems function well, they provide so many services that support humans at the same time, like food and nutrient recycling. I feel this is evidence of God's provision for the needs of the whole system. This is a type of purpose."

Working in conservation can be discouraging, but Margaret derives hope from the good news that there is a God who cares about us and has his own interest in maintaining these ecosystems. At the end of the flood story in Genesis, God says he will never allow such complete devastation to happen again. God didn't make this promise just to Noah and his family, but he also included "every living creature". Seeing examples like this of God's concern for the whole world gives Margaret hope that she is taking part in something much bigger than herself, and that it will ultimately succeed – though we also need to play our part. Two passages from the Bible resonate particularly well with Margaret:

> But the basic reality of God is plain enough. Open your eyes and there it is! By taking a long and thoughtful look at what God has created, people have always been able to see what their eyes as such can't see: eternal power, for instance, and the mystery of his divine being. So nobody has a good excuse.
> **Romans 1:19-20 (MSG)**

You can be sure that God will take care of everything you
need, his generosity exceeding even yours in the glory
that pours from Jesus.
Philippians 4:19 (MSG)

Reflections

My own perspective on the living world has been influenced by
Hilary Marlow, a biblical scholar who is a tutor and fellow of Girton
College, Cambridge. Hilary often points out that the world was not
created by God purely for our benefit. She is interested in what the
Bible has to say about God's relationship with and purposes for the
whole of creation – both human and non-human.

For example, Psalm 104 focuses on God's goodness and creativity,
praising him and celebrating the wonder and diversity of everything
he has made. There are hints in this psalm of an understanding of
habitats and food chains. People and their activities are specifically
mentioned in only four of the thirty-five verses. Everything in
creation, both human and non-human, depends on God and is
important to him.

How many are your works, Lord!
In wisdom you made them all;
the earth is full of your creatures.
There is the sea, vast and spacious,
teeming with creatures beyond number –
living things both large and small.
There the ships go to and fro,
and Leviathan, which you formed to frolic there.
Psalm 104:24–26 (NIV)

The Bible makes clear that the ultimate purpose of all creation is to
praise and worship God. It's fairly obvious how human beings can
worship God if they choose, but what about everything else? The
writers of the psalms, Hilary says, don't seem very concerned with
describing exactly how rocks or trees are praising God. They are too
busy celebrating the fact that it is happening.

Perhaps creation praises God simply by being its diverse and wonderful self and fulfilling the task for which it was made. In this way, creation points toward God, helping people to worship and honour him. Psalm 19 is probably the most well-loved example of this.

> The heavens declare the glory of God;
> the skies proclaim the work of his hands.
> Day after day they pour forth speech;
> night after night they reveal knowledge.
> They have no speech, they use no words;
> no sound is heard from them.
> Yet their voice goes out into all the earth,
> their words to the ends of the world.
> **Psalm 19:1–4 (NIV)**

The living world can only fulfil its purposes if it has the right conditions to flourish, as the work of people like Margaret Miller (Chapter 8) has demonstrated over the last few decades. Damage to one part of an ecosystem can have far-reaching effects on the surrounding land and on all of its human and non-human inhabitants.

Although the biblical writers didn't have all the modern-day understanding of science that we enjoy, they were very clear about cause and effect, and the interconnectedness of all of life. Hilary believes that the Bible paints a picture of a relationship between God, people, and the rest of creation that can be visualized as a series of close connections.

The overall picture painted by the Bible is of a richly woven and interconnected world that has value and purpose, both now and for the future, where humankind is commanded to "serve and preserve" creation. That picture is fully compatible with the findings of modern science. The goodness of creation is also an encouragement to do science well, releasing us to explore the living world in a responsible way, reflecting on the questions about meaning and purpose that our research raises for humankind.

The leading seventeenth-century botanist John Ray found that Christian faith inspired him to take science seriously, and in return science enhanced his faith. Three centuries later, this kind of input from faith to science and back again is still happening. The people described in this book come from different scientific disciplines, each of which has its own techniques, fascinations, and ways of assessing data. Their journeys into faith were also different, and they relate to God in their own ways – although they have the same core beliefs in common.

Each one of these researchers believes that science and faith can work together. They want to see evidence to back up their commitments and are willing to face up to the truth of reality. This level of honesty requires some humility, but it is also hopeful. Who knows what's around the corner, just waiting to be discovered! As Rhoda Hawkins has said, "One of the reasons I went into science in the first place is because of my belief in God, but it also goes the other way. The more I study the world around me... the more that shows me something of the creator God. So studying science strengthens my faith, and my faith strengthens my motivation to do science."

Their work is influenced by their Christian beliefs in different ways, whether it feeds directly into the scientific questions they are asking, the projects they choose to work on, or their approach to asking difficult questions. For some, their faith is deeply affected by their science. For others, like Jeff Hardin, the influence has gone more the other way. "The joy of discovery is also the joy of appreciating the world that God has made... Understanding in a way that no one else has actually ever understood... leads me to thank God for the amazing world that we have to enjoy and to explore." I hope you, too, have enjoyed wondering at the living world.

Acknowledgements

This book would not have been completed without the help of many people. The six scientists and two theologians involved gave advice, patiently read and corrected drafts, spoke at a conference, were filmed, and generally gave of themselves for very little reward except the privilege of communicating their work to a general audience. Cara Parrett was a wonderful, resourceful research assistant who brought her own valuable experience and a whole range of skills to the project.

I would also like to thank everyone at Lion Hudson whose passion for the idea of this book and hard work played a very significant role in turning it into a reality. Particular thanks go to my editors, Jessica Gladwell and Rebecca Bradshaw, who went way beyond the call of duty to make this book happen, and to help me shape it into its final form. Another Lion author, David Hutchings, kindly taught me how to make a scientific chapter into a story.

This project was carried out at The Faraday Institute for Science and Religion, Cambridge, where the other directors made it possible for me to do this work, and the entire staff gave support, advice, and assistance in many important ways.

A number of people provided advice at the beginning of the project and/or feedback on drafts, including Denis Alexander, Trevor Allan, Poppy and Phil Balding, the staff of BioLogos, Justin Brierley, Guilherme de Carvalho, Andrew Chamberlain, Nicholas Condie, Wendy Daneel, Pablo de Felipe, Keith Fox, Nick Green, Lizzie Henderson, Rodney Holder, Bethany Johnson, Ard Louis, Nathan Lyons, Alexander Maßmann, Glenn Myers, Michael Ramsden, Michael Reiss, Rachel Simonson, John Spicer, Bob Storey, David Vosburg, and Rebecca Watson. The final text represents my own views, not necessarily the views of those mentioned here, and any mistakes that remain are my own. So many people have helped in the production of this book that I must apologize to anyone who has been inadvertently missed off the list.

This work was funded by a grant from the Templeton World Charity Foundation.

Further Reading:
how to stay informed

The website **wondersofthelivingworld.org** is packed full of resources to help you explore these ideas in more depth, including articles, videos, notes for church-based study groups (adults), and material for UK secondary school teachers.

Websites

faraday.cam.ac.uk: High-quality resources and information from the Faraday Institute: short papers, audio, videos, courses, and more.

cis.org.uk: Christians in Science, the UK-based network for those concerned with the relationship between science and Christian faith. Links to similar organizations around the world can be found at cis. org.uk/resources/.

biologos.org: A US-based organization that invites the church and the world to see the harmony between science and biblical faith as it presents an evolutionary understanding of God's creation. Excellent and very accessible blogs, articles, videos, and more.

Books

Denis Alexander, *Creation or Evolution: Do We Have to Choose?* 2nd Edition (Oxford: Monarch, 2014). An in-depth look at the issue of whether a faithful reading of biblical teaching on creation is compatible with current evolutionary biology.

Denis Alexander, *Is There Purpose in Biology?: The Cost of Existence and the God of Love* (Oxford: Monarch, 2018). Addresses the claim that evolution is random and obviously without purpose, suggesting that the biological evidence itself does not support such a claim.

Ruth M. Bancewicz, *Test of FAITH: Spiritual Journeys with Scientists* (Bletchley: Authentic, 2009). Ten scientists tell their stories about their Christian faith, their careers in science, and how the two fit together. Includes Francis Collins, John Polkinghorne, and Alister McGrath.

Ruth M. Bancewicz, *God in the Lab: How Science Enhances Faith* (Oxford: Monarch, 2015). Stories of creativity, imagination, beauty, wonder, and awe in both science and faith. With contributions from six scientists, including Rhoda Hawkins and Jeff Hardin.

R. J. Berry (Editor), *The Lion Handbook of Science and Christianity* (Oxford: Lion, 2012). With contributions from many of the leading lights in the UK science and faith discussion, this colour illustrated book is a great introduction to all the main issues.

Sean B. Carroll, *Endless Forms Most Beautiful: The New Science of Evo Devo* (London: Weidenfeld & Nicholson, 2006). Exploring the recent revolution in understanding how animals develop and evolve. Carroll is a great teacher and a lyrical writer whose love of his subject shines through.

Alan Chapman, *Slaying the Dragons: Destroying Myths in the History of Science and Faith* (Oxford: Lion, 2013). Drawing on contemporary sources, this approachable book shows that the history of science and of faith always have been closely intertwined.

Simon Conway Morris, *The Crucible of Creation: The Burgess Shale and the Rise of Animals* (Oxford: Oxford University Press, 1998). A fascinating short summary of the Burgess Shale discoveries and their implications for science.

Larry Gonick and Mark Wheelis, *The Cartoon Guide to Genetics, Updated edition* (New York: Harper Perennial, 1991). Amusing and easy-to-grasp introduction to the biology of the genetic code. Or Aysha Divan and Janice A. Royds, *Molecular Biology: A Very Short Introduction* (Oxford: Oxford University Press, 2016).

Rodney Holder, *Big Bang Big God: A Universe Designed for Life?* (Oxford: Lion, 2013). An introduction to the science behind the origin of the universe, fine-tuning arguments, and the disputed concept of a multiverse.

David Hutchings and Tom McLeish, *Let There Be Science: Why God Loves Science, and Science Needs God* (Oxford: Lion, 2017). Using stories about science and the biblical story of Job, this book shows how science flourishes in a Christian setting.

Ernest Lucas, *Can We Believe Genesis Today?* (London: IVP, 2005). An introduction to the main issues in interpreting Genesis, written by a biblical scholar who was formerly a biochemist.

Hilary Marlow, *The Earth is the Lord's: A Biblical Response to Environmental Issues* (Grove Biblical Series, 2008). A short, readable, and relevant summary of some of Hilary's work on the Bible and environmental ethics.

Alister E. McGrath, *Inventing the Universe: Why We Can't Stop Talking about Science, Faith and God* (London: Hodder & Stoughton, 2015). One of Alister's most recent popular-level books on the relationship between science and faith.

Martin Nowak with Roger Highfield, *Super Cooperators: Altrusim,*

Evolution and Why We Need Each Other to Succeed (Edinburgh: Canongate, 2012). An accessible summary of Nowak's work on mathematical biology.

Samir Okasha, *Philosophy of Science: A Very Short Introduction* (Oxford: Oxford University Press, 2002). Essential reading for science students, as well as those getting involved in the science and religion dialogue.

John Polkinghorne, *Quarks, Chaos and Christianity: Questions to Science and Religion* (New York: Crossroad, 2005). One of the leading lights in the science and religion dialogue explains how both science and faith point to something greater than ourselves.

Forest Rohwer with Merry Youle, with illustrations by Derek Vosten, *Coral Reefs in the Microbial Seas* (Plaid Press, 2010). Fascinating, accessible, and at times humorous. A beautifully illustrated look at the complex world of the coral reef, and its threats.

Peter D. Ward and Donald Brownlee, *Rare Earth: Why Complex Life is Uncommon in the Universe* (New York: Springer, 2009). Exploring the reasons why microbial life may be common in the universe, while animal life may be rare.

Tom Wright, *Simply Christian* (London: SPCK, 2006). The biblical scholar N. T. Wright explains the essentials of Christianity in his usual highly readable and rational style, drawing on the themes of justice, beauty, and love.

Glossary

Words in bold refer to other glossary entries.

Actin: A type of **protein**. Lots of actin **molecules** can join together like a string of beads to make long filaments which support and move the cell around, and help with transport within the cell. Actin filaments are part of the **cell**'s inner skeleton, called the **cytoskeleton**, which is found in all living organisms more complex than bacteria.

Algae: A very diverse group of plants. Includes seaweeds, as well as many single-celled types. Algae are mainly aquatic, make their own energy from the sun, and have no true roots, stems, or leaves.

Amino acids: Small **molecules** that are joined together in long chains to make large **protein** molecules. Each amino acid has the same central structure, with a side chain giving it unique properties.

Atom: The smallest unit of matter (atoms can be broken into smaller pieces but this is destructive, releasing charged particles), e.g. hydrogen, helium, oxygen, carbon, nitrogen. Also known as **chemical elements**, which are described in the **periodic table**.

Big Bang: The beginning of the universe as we know it, which started in a very hot, condensed state. At a point known as a singularity, the condensed stuff expanded very rapidly, and time and space came into existence. In the first few minutes, particles began to come together to form hydrogen, helium, and lithium.

Much later, these **atoms** then came together to form stars, which produced all the other **chemical elements**.

Biochemistry: The study of the chemicals that make up living things.

Cell: The building block of living things. A cell has a thin outer membrane, with a syrupy mixture of **molecules** and microscopic structures inside. The only human cell that is visible to the naked eye is the egg cell. A bacterium consists of a single, relatively simple cell. Every other living thing is made of one or more complex cells, which have internal compartments.

Chemical elements: The **atoms** that can be joined together to make **molecules**.

Chromosome: A naturally occurring, relatively long section of **DNA**, which is coiled into a neat package when the cell divides. Humans have forty-six chromosomes: twenty-two pairs, plus either XY or XX in males or females.

Convergent evolution: The observation that evolutionary processes tend to hit upon similar solutions to similar problems. For example, structures like the camera eye, wings, and certain **enzymes** have evolved independently multiple times.

Creation: The Christian belief that the universe and everything in it was made by God. Within Christianity there are multiple interpretations of the creation account in the book of Genesis and how this fits with the science. The contributors to this book believe that Genesis is a theological, not scientific, account of creation, which is compatible with modern scientific accounts.

Cytoskeleton: A collection of different types of thin filament that support the **cell**, act as train tracks for transporting things around inside, and can also move the cell around.

Developmental biology: The study of how living organisms develop from a single fertilized egg.

DNA: Deoxyribonucleic acid, a long, thin **molecule** made from multiple copies of the four molecular building blocks: adenine, thymine, cytosine, and guanine (A, T, C, and G), arranged in a precise order. The sequence of these units contains the **cell**'s information for building **proteins** and for controlling where and when they are made.

Double helix: The two strands of the **DNA molecule** are shaped like a spiral staircase, which is known as a double helix.

Ecology: The study of ecosystems.

Ecosystem: A combined community of plants, animals, and other organisms, together with the non-living factors they interact with, such as air, water, and rock.

Elements: See atoms or chemical elements.

Enzyme: A class of **proteins** which can act as catalysts, speeding up the rate of chemical reactions.

Evolution: The process by which populations of organisms change over very long periods of time. **Mutations** in **genes** cause changes in the bodies of different individuals. If a particular mutation helps organisms to live and thrive together in their environment, it is more likely to be passed on to the next generation, and will eventually spread throughout the population.

Game theory: A mathematical method for studying situations that involve a series of interdependent decisions and their consequences. A classic example is the prisoner's dilemma, where a pair of criminals are isolated and questioned by the police. The prisoners need to guess whether the best course of action is to lie or tell the truth, depending on the penalties or rewards, and what their colleague is most likely to do. Game theory is used in a range of practical situations, including economics, politics, and business.

Gene: A section of **DNA** which codes for a **protein**, including the regions that regulate where and when it is produced.

Genesis: The first book of the Bible. The first two chapters of Genesis contain two of the main creation stories in the Bible.

Genetic code: The way in which **DNA** contains information about how to build a **protein**. Each of the twenty **amino acids** used to make proteins are represented by a three-letter DNA code word, which is made up of three of the four DNA subunits (A, G, C, and T). There are 64 possible DNA code words, so each amino acid is represented by several different words.

Genetics: The study of how physical characteristics are inherited from one generation to another, and how they vary among populations.

Haemoglobin: The **protein** in red blood cells that carries oxygen around the body.

Hormone: A type of **molecule** (such as **insulin** or adrenaline) which carries a signal from one part of the body to another.

Incarnation: The event in which Christians believe the Son of God took on human form in the person of Jesus Christ.

Insulin: A **hormone** produced by the pancreas, which tells liver, muscle, and fat cells to start extracting sugar from the bloodstream, where it can be stored or used as a source of energy.

Keratin: A type of **protein** found in hair, fingernails, claws, horns, beaks, feathers, scales, and turtle shells, and which gives strength and waterproof properties to the outer layer of skin.

Laws of physics: Matter and energy behave in predictable ways that can be described by simple 'laws'. The physical laws include the speed of light, gravity, the forces within an **atom**, and the behaviour of gases under certain conditions.

Microtubule: Part of the **cell**'s inner skeleton (the **cytoskeleton**). Microtubules are made of subunits called tubulin, and help support the cell and move its contents around.

Molecule: An arrangement of **atoms**, joined together by chemical bonds. Smaller molecules can join together with the same types of chemical bonds to make larger molecules.

Mutation: A change in the sequence of **DNA** subunits. Causes can include a spelling mistake when DNA is copied from one **cell** to another, chemical damage, or radiation.

Nerve: A type of **cell** in the body, also called a neuron or neurone. A nerve cell receives electrical signals at one end, conducts them down its thin 'axon' (which can be very long), and transmits them at the other end to another nerve or part of the body through structures called synapses.

New Testament: The last twenty-seven books of the Bible, which were written after the time of Christ.

Nucleus: The central hub of the **cell**. Here, **DNA** is stored and copied, so the information contained in the **genes** can be delivered to the rest of the cell for making **proteins**.

Old Testament: The first thirty-nine books of the Bible, which were written before the time of Christ.

Ordination: The process by which individuals are formally consecrated or commissioned as clergy in a particular Christian denomination.

Palaeobiology: The study of fossilized organisms.

Parasite: An organism that lives off another living thing, giving nothing back in return, and sometimes damaging its host in the process.

Periodic table: A way of organizing all known **chemical elements** (types of **atom**) that makes sense of their various structures and properties. When the elements are listed in order of atomic number (roughly equivalent to weight order), a recurring pattern of chemical properties emerges. When the atomic list is broken up into a table, these properties run down the columns.

Plankton: Small organisms that drift in water (either salt or freshwater), below the surface. Includes plants, bacteria, **algae**, crustaceans, molluscs, and the eggs and larvae of many marine animals.

Platelet: A type of blood **cell** found in mammals, which is formed in the bone marrow and stored in the spleen. When a blood vessel is punctured, platelets clump together in the gap, providing a surface on which the blood clot can form.

Protein: A type of large **molecule** made from a chain of **amino acids**. Each protein chain folds into a precise three-dimensional shape. Proteins do work in the body, such as carrying oxygen, sending a signal, acting as enzymes, or forming structures like **actin** or tubulin.

Random: When used in a scientific sense, this means unpredictable. The most probable outcome could be predicted mathematically, using statistics, but a single random event cannot be predicted with complete accuracy.

Stem cell: A type of **cell** that can multiply indefinitely. Embryonic stem cells can contribute to any tissue in the body. Adult stem cells have a more limited repertoire of cell types.

Translation: In a biological sense, this is the process in which a **gene** is used to make a **protein**. A section of **DNA** is first copied into a similar **molecule** called RNA in the nucleus. That RNA is exported from the **nucleus** and translated into a string of **amino acids**, by a set of molecular machines, to generate the protein.

Trilobite: A type of arthropod (the family of animals that includes insects, spiders, and crabs) that was common between 521 and around 250–252 million years ago. One of the longest-surviving animal groups, and relatively easy to find in fossil beds all over the world.

Fig 1: A normal animal cell. In reality the contents are usually more tightly packed than this, but this simplified diagram shows the different types of sub-compartments.

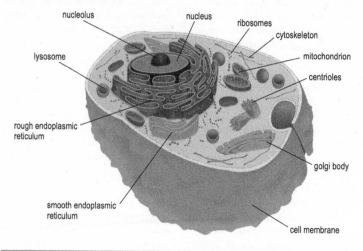

Fig 2: A DNA strand is unwound and a copy is made of one of its genes. That copy is then translated into protein, inside a translating machine (which is itself made of protein) called a ribosome.

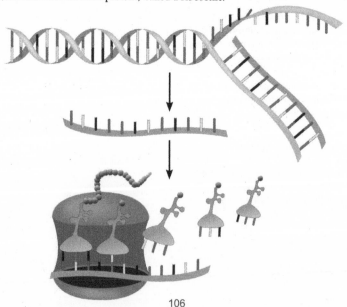

Fig 3: The genetic code.

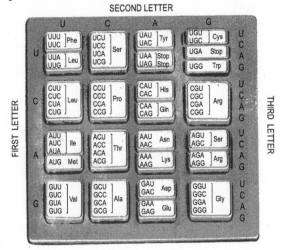

Fig 4: Actin filaments move a bit like a caterpillar track: subunits are constantly adding on and dropping off both ends. More are added at the plus end and they drop off more frequently from the minus end, so the overall effect is that the filament moves along in one direction.

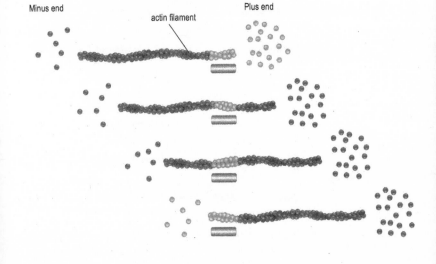

Fig 5: A motor protein moves cargo around the cell by "walking" along the cell's inner skeleton.

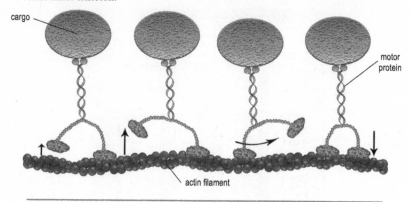

cargo

motor protein

actin filament

Fig 6: Motor proteins make a muscle contract by "walking" along actin filaments in opposite directions, pulling them closer together,

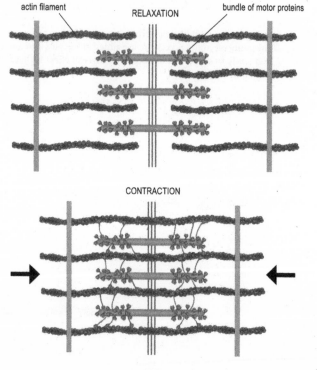

actin filament

RELAXATION

bundle of motor proteins

CONTRACTION

Fig 7: The embryo begins to form in week three. A ridge develops where two layers of cells meet, through which cells dive down to create a middle layer. The ridge deepens and closes over, as the triple layer of cells curls up and takes shape into an embryo.

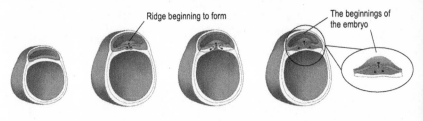

Ridge beginning to form

The beginnings of the embryo

Fig 8: A coral polyp.

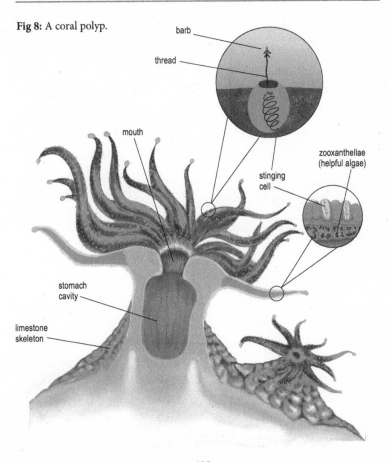

barb

thread

mouth

zooxanthellae (helpful algae)

stinging cell

stomach cavity

limestone skeleton

Fig 9: The elkhorn coral life-cycle.

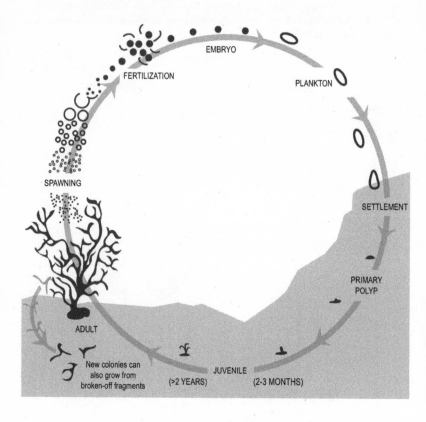